National Movement and Empowerment of Women

National Movement and Empowerment of Women

Nation-Building in the United Provinces

Malabika Pande

RAWAT PUBLICATIONS

Jaipur • New Delhi • Bangalore • Guwahati • Kolkata

ISBN 978-81-316-0878-4

Published by
Prem Rawat for **Rawat Publications**
Satyam Apts, Sector 3, Jawahar Nagar, Jaipur 302 004 (India)
Phone: 0141 265 1748 / 7006 Fax: 0141 265 1748
E-mail: info@rawatbooks.com
Website: www.rawatbooks.com

New Delhi Office
4858/24, Ansari Road, Daryaganj, New Delhi 110 002
Phone: 011 2326 3290

Also at *Bangalore, Guwahati* and *Kolkata*

Typeset by Logiciels Info Solutions, Chennai
Printed at Chaman Enterprises, New Delhi

To all those women,
known and unknown,
who make us proud of our past.

Contents

Preface

Work on this book began as a result of a UGC Post-doctoral Research Project I was awarded in 1995. Initially the subject was 'Education and Political Mobilisation of Women in the United Provinces, 1916–1942', but as the project metamorphosed into a book, the scope and subject matter expanded considerably.

Right from the initial stage, my supervisor, Prof. Rekha Joshi, Head of the Department of Medieval and Modern History, University of Allahabad, helped me by giving me full liberty to experiment with my own ideas. I have chosen four districts in UP, namely Allahabad, Lucknow, Agra and Almora, which represent the eastern, central, western and northern regions respectively, for detailed study. This gives a fairly representative picture of women's political activism during the most active phase of the freedom movement in the Provinces. In each of the districts I was helped enormously by local contact persons, libraries and archives.

The Nehru Memorial Museum and Library in New Delhi has invaluable material for the kind of research I did and I took considerable help from it, especially the 'Old Newspapers Section' and the 'Microfilm Department'.

The National Archives in Delhi had to be visited to check Home Department Files and Fortnightly Reports of the Government. It has vast resources and helpful staff who go out of their way to help research scholars.

The material of legislative proceedings of the United Provinces Legislative Assembly, which was relevant to my study, was found in the Central Library of Banaras Hindu University. The Government Records Section in the Manuscript Department of the Library has valuable source material which needs to be digitised for its own protection. The process of digitisation has now begun.

My family and friends, particularly my husband Vinaya, provided invaluable help and support in the writing of book, for which I am deeply indebted to them.

Malabika Pande

Introduction

Historians, generally speaking, have not recognized the major role played by women in India's struggle for freedom from British rule. While scholars do tend to agree that the participation of women led to their own emancipation, many do not in clear terms acknowledge their conspicuous role in the liberation of the country.[1] Thus, the erudite scholar Gyanendra Pandey, in his excellent monograph on the ascendancy of the Congress in the United Provinces (now, Uttar Pradesh) in the 1920s and 1930s,[2] has not devoted even a single paragraph to the issue, and the celebrated historian Bipan Chandra has also not highlighted this aspect in his magnum opus on India's struggle for freedom.[3]

The link between education and political activity is self-evident and has been recognized as such the world over. In British India, till the early decades of the twentieth century, the United Provinces lagged behind the Presidencies of Bengal, Bombay and Madras in respect of the growth of education and political organizations. There are several explorations on the linkage between education and the political mobilization of women in the three Presidencies, but the United Provinces have only recently begun to attract attention on this score.[4] There was therefore a need for an examination that particularly focused on the spread of women's education and political mobilization in the United Provinces.

The three Presidencies came under direct British rule several decades earlier than the United Provinces. Also, the indigenous education system, though vigorous in some other parts of the country, was generally in a state of crisis on the eve of British rule in the areas eventually amalgamated to form the United Provinces. This indigenous system underwent further decline on account of the revenue policies of the British administration and its general outlook towards 'native' endeavours. Moreover, a modern educational set-up instituted or aided by the State, particularly at the elementary and secondary levels, grew very slowly as it was never a priority for the colonial administration despite pious declarations to the contrary. As a result, there came into being an educational vacuum in the United Provinces. Added to this was the fact that women's education had already been neglected on account of social attitudes towards it even before British rule, hence this vacuum impinged more severely on the meagre educational resources available for girls. The British administration seemed to be in consonance with the patriarchal social outlook of its subjects in this respect. This was consistently reflected in the wide disparity in literacy levels between men and women in successive Census reports.

Obviously, the educational status of women was not homogeneous across social and class barriers, and, in general, attitudes towards women's education and their actual attainments in this regard were relatively more affirmative in the affluent sections of the urban areas. Moreover, the aggregate picture was one of social and educational stagnation of women. This had a natural impact on the participation of women in public life in general and the nationalist movement in particular. From the early stages of national mobilization, leading figures of the movements for social reform and national emancipation like Ram Mohun Roy, Isvar Chandra Vidyasagar, Dayanand Saraswati, Jyotiba Phule, Gopal Hari Deshmukh, G.V. Joshi, G.G. Agarkar, Pandita Ramabai and many more, regretted this state of affairs and called for educational and other efforts to bring women into the social and national mainstream, and endow them with equal agency and opportunities to the extent possible in a patriarchal social setup.[5]

As nationalist activity gained momentum in the region from the end of the 1880s, the exclusively male composition of politics was apparent, with not even a token representation of women. The question was not simply of the poor spread of female education; it had a more complex character – the underlying factors were related to popular perceptions about women's status in society. However, by the end of the first decade of the twentieth century, some elements of change became manifest albeit mainly in respect of urban elite groups that typically comprised the traditional literati who had benefited from – and to a certain extent contributed to – the expansion of Anglo-Vernacular and English education.

Though a microscopic minority, girls belonging to the three traditionally literate groups in the United Provinces, that is upper-class Muslims, the Kayastha community and the somewhat socially diverse adherents of the reformist *Arya Samaj*, did manage to get educated to some extent despite the shortcomings and inadequacies typical to a regressive social situation as prevalent in the territory. In Muslim households there were *purdah* restrictions too; hence, whatever education was available was to be had only indoors as girls were strictly prohibited from venturing out of their homes, let alone going out to pursue education. Girls in Muslim households were encouraged to learn enough Arabic to enable them to read the Koran but were discouraged from learning to write because of the fear that they would then transgress the prescribed limits. As Gail Minault has observed in her notable study on the education of Muslim women in Colonial India: 'For a woman to know how to write was dangerous. If women had power over the written word, their capacity to disrupt men's lives would be increased.'[6] Bi-Amman, the mother of the Ali brothers (Maulana Mohammad Ali and Maulana Shaukat Ali), was one such woman who clandestinely learnt to read Urdu in order to enjoy a popular Urdu novel.[7]

Girls of the Kayastha community were also privileged with opportunities for education, even if to a lesser extent *vis-à-vis* boys. The famous poetess of Allahabad, Mahadevi Verma (born in 1902 or 1908, according to different versions), happened to be a particularly fortunate member of this community. Her father taught English at a college near Indore and believed in educating all his children irrespective of their sex. Though married at the age of nine, and despite many other social obstacles, she was able to study up to M.A., which she completed in 1933. She was one of only two girls in her class.[8]

The Arya Samaj Movement though based in Punjab had considerable impact nationwide on women's social and political mobilization. The Kanya Mahavidyalaya (KMV hereinafter) of Jalandhar, founded in 1896 by Lala Devaraj (a leading figure of the Arya Samaj), was the foremost institution in this regard. Lala Devaraj's belief was that 'when mothers will become *Aryas*, why would then sons not be good *Aryas*?' For Lala Devaraj, the nation's prime strength was in *Matri Shakti* (mother-power). From the beginning, the founders of KMV endeavoured to widen the scope of girls' education and keep it above sectarian concerns, 'in spite of their links with and roots in the Hindu chauvinist Arya Samaj ideology'.[9] By 1910, there were nine girls from Baluchistan, six from the Frontier Provinces, 27 from the United Provinces; one from south India (Hyderabad), six from Burma, three from Rajputana, two from Sindh, one each from Bombay, Assam and Bengal and 98 from Punjab. Soon after, girls started coming from as far as Fiji and Africa.[10]

A significant aspect of the KMV model was the formation of a women's association (the *Stri Samaj*) with units all over Punjab, each with women preachers, called *Pracharikas*. These associations focused on the regeneration of society by the educational and social empowerment of women. The *Pracharikas* travelled not only in Punjab but also in other provinces all over India, speaking to big audiences and raising funds for their cause. Lala Devaraj often accompanied them. Prominent among these women were Mai Bhagwati, Savitri, Lajjyawati, Devaki Devi and Narayani Devi. The United Provinces was often part of their itinerary. Shanno Devi even travelled to Burma and Africa. In those days (between 1900 and 1935), public speaking and travelling were very much male domains. KMV women and girls thus broke new ground in this aspect of their work. The impact of these travelling preachers may be estimated from their effect on Sarojini Naidu, who, Kishwar states, 'is supposed to have acknowledged that she was inspired to take to public speaking after having heard Savitri speak'. The calibre of Savitri received appropriate recognition in 1913, when she became the first woman Principal of KMV.[11]

At a time of national turmoil, popular literature may also have a stirring impact. This was the case in the United Provinces too, with the advent of Munshi Premchand's works in popular literature and nationalist discourse, which were key catalysts in stirring nationalist sentiments. His zeal for women's education and evoking a spirit of sacrifice for the nation in female teachers is reflected in *Rahasya*. In this story, Vimal Prakash, an idealistic, public spirited young man sets up Sevashram, a school for poor girls in Benares; after great difficulty, he finds a female teacher willing to teach for a very meagre sum, even though her husband was a well-paid bank employee in Lucknow.[12] Premchand's *Aahuti*, written in 1930, is a story of three university students, Anand, Vishambhar and Rupmani, who were forced to make a choice between their career and fighting for the country's freedom. Rupmani is shown to support Vishambhar who joins the national struggle for freedom and gets imprisoned for two years. The purpose of education, says Rupmani, is not to earn degrees but the ability to build strength of character.[13] Rupmani represented the new generation of womanhood that was emerging in the United Provinces at this time. Premchand's popularity and impact as a writer may be gauged from the fact that his novels and stories have been translated in all the major languages not only of India but also of the world.

Nationalist concern with the universalization of primary education and the government's own policy decisions in this regard called for special emphasis on female educational advancement, though there was a great deal of equivocation on its nature and content. Meanwhile, the momentum gathered by the nationalist movement itself created opportunities for women's participation in public life which, in turn, catalysed female education. From the early 1920s, particularly under Gandhi's leadership, the nationalist movement began to make conscious efforts to mobilize women, not merely for activities under Gandhi's Constructive Programme but also for mainline political activity.

As hinted earlier, the increasing presence of women in the public domain in the subsequent decades had a self-fulfilling impact on women's education even in areas where such presence did not seem to have a direct link with the existing status of female education. However, the actual levels of expansion in this sphere were to a large extent subject to other kinds of constraints – financial as well as social. The rate of growth of female education, the levels of continuing enrolment of girls in schools, the functional significance assigned to literacy and the social value of being educated, all displayed throughout the period from the 1920s severe disparities in the agency and power extended to males and females. Indian women were clearly not one among equals in a society that was dominated by patriarchy. Yet, it would be incorrect to discount the signal role of education in the promotion of women's participation in public life. The present study seeks to examine the actualities in respect of the linkage of education with the political mobilization of women, with particular reference to elementary and secondary education in the period from 1916 (heightening of mass nationalist activity) to 1942 (the *Quit India* Movement).

The study is based upon official as well as non-official sources and other private and public documentary materials and transcripts of interviews recorded by me or, in some cases, by my teacher Dr Uma Rao with women activists, very few of whom are alive, or their close relatives or with people who are well-informed about the times. What is noteworthy is that the women activists were often from the middle and lower middle classes and not all had husbands who were co-participants in the movement; some of the women joined the movement in spite of their husbands' opposition.[14] Many were widows or single and only slightly educated in the formal sense.

Some ground realities regarding the United Provinces have to be mentioned in order to place the issue in its proper context. The material poverty of the Province was acknowledged by the British administration itself in several official publications, the last being the Report (1945) of the John Woodhead Commission on the disastrous Bengal Famine of 1943.[15] Female literacy in India was at an abysmal low, at 2.9 per cent in 1931,[16] and the United Provinces presented a more dismal picture in this regard, the manifest result of studied neglect by the British administration over a very long period.[17]

Added to this were the glaring disabilities of Indian women of the time; these included problems of dowry, widow remarriage, general oppression and stigmatization of widows, and lack of inheritance rights and education. The subservient position of women was enforced by confining women to specific domestic roles, often resulting in their complete seclusion. Another major obstacle to women's participation in the public domain was the more or less universal attitude of patriarchy, that women and their honour were the bases of family esteem, which could not be put at risk for the sake of giving personal space to women.[18]

A factor mentioned by Gyanendra Pandey in the monograph cited earlier may have had some effect in spreading social consciousness and increasing political opportunities in the United Provinces. This was the passing of two constitutional innovations, namely, the U.P. Municipalities Act of 1916 and the U.P. District Boards Act of 1922, which extended the franchise and the powers of the municipalities.[19] Another important factor was that in the division of subjects under Dyarchy (as instituted by the Government of India Act, 1919) education became a Provincial subject. This coincided with the beginning of mass mobilization during the *Khilafat* and Non-Cooperation Movement, 1920–1922, which called for the boycott of government schools and colleges and setting up of national institutions.

A slight increase in the number of recognized educational institutions in the urban areas was recorded in the 1920s, and the number of universities rose to five in 1927 in the United Provinces. The United Provinces in any case presents a paradox in being one of the more backward states in India and at the same time in the forefront of the freedom struggle.[20]

Since all the women activists I have interviewed and the documentary material I have studied bear the unmistakable impact of Mohandas Karamchand Gandhi, it will not be out of place to briefly examine what he was saying and doing and how his messages were being conveyed to different parts of the provinces and indeed of the country during that period. Gandhi's regard for women as equal partners of men both in private and public life was the outcome of his experiences in *satyagraha* in South Africa particularly in the last phase, that is, between 1913 and 1914. Most of the Indian women there were poor and illiterate, yet they proved their ability to sacrifice their all for their own and their country's honour.[21] The condition of most women in India at the time was no different. Therefore, from the beginning of his public life in India, Gandhi was determined to bring home to the people the message and importance of women's mobilization and their latent capacities for struggle and sacrifice.

In 1917 at the Gujarat Political Conference in Godhra he said: 'We have kept our women away from these activities of ours and have thus become victims of a kind of paralysis. The nation walks with one leg only.'[22] This message was repeated at every public meeting Gandhi addressed till the end of his life. Beginning with the Rowlatt *Satyagraha* in April 1919, he appealed to the women of India to cooperate with the men and join the Satyagraha movement in large numbers.[23] His appeals for funds in cash or kind or for practising and propagating *Swadeshi* were stated as religious or traditional duties towards the motherland.[24] He also highlighted the fact that spinning Khadi yarn could serve as a vital mechanism for the economic emancipation of needy women[25] while providing a means to better-off women and men to identify themselves with the less privileged in society on one hand, and leading the country towards self-reliance in cotton production on the other. Just after launching the Salt Satyagraha on 6 April 1930, Gandhi issued a special appeal in his weekly *Young India*, to the women of India to take up the work of picketing and spinning (dated 10 April 1930). This was carried in the national and local newspapers across the country. 'The effect was almost miraculous,'[26] writes R.C. Majumdar, and produced a chain reaction, spurring the men on towards greater effort. As Jawaharlal Nehru noted: 'Generally the attitude of the women was more unyielding than that of the men. Often they became Congress "dictators" in provinces and local areas.'[27]

Gandhi's statements, speeches and activities were, apart from being carried in his own publications *Young India* and *Navajivan*, faithfully reported in the newspapers and journals of the country. Not only were these, particularly the papers in the regional languages, cheap and thus widely accessible (e.g. the daily *Aaj* of Varanasi cost only 2 paisa in the 1930s!) but also had a much larger reach as they were 'read to illiterate hearers by their literate fellows in town, villages, railway carriages, public meetings and so on'.[28] The circulation of the Hindi monthly *Chaand* published from Allahabad went up from 8,000 in 1927 to 15,000 in 1930, and of the Hindi weekly *Pratap* published from Kanpur also went up from 7,800 to 16,000 during the same period. About the impact of *Chaand* it would be worthwhile to quote the celebrated freedom fighter and social and cultural activist Kamaladevi Chattopadhyay: 'There is no doubt that *Chaand* is playing a very important role in the literary and social renaissance of the country; is also contributing not a little for the progress of the women's cause by its steady championship. I am not surprised it has endeared itself to so many of our women folk.'[29]

Political resolutions, messages and news-sheets were often issued from the local Congress offices and as soon as they were banned by the government they were handwritten, cyclostyled or copied and distributed quite efficiently over a wide area.[30] Nationalist songs, poems and slogans were composed during this period and formed an inevitable part of daily processions and demonstrations; thus, a composition popular all over the United Provinces was:

Hai avtaar Mahatma Gandhi ka
Bharat azad karane ko
Sri Ram ke kar me dhanua tha
Sri Krishna ke kar me murli thi
Gandhi ke kar me charkha hai
Bharat azad karane ko.[31]

A free translation of the above lines would be:

Mahatma Gandhi has been born
To make India free
Lord Ram had the bow in his hand
Lord Krishna had the flute in his hand
Gandhi has the spinning wheel in his hand
To make India free.

NOTES

1. For a discussion on the perceptions of participants and conclusions of scholars on this issue, see: (i) Suruchi Thapar-Bjorkert, *Women in the Indian National Movement: Unseen Faces and Unheard Voices, 1930–42*. New Delhi: Sage Publications India, 2006, pp. 43–47; (ii) Geraldine Forbes, *Women in Modern India* (*Vol.IV.2: The New Cambridge History of India*). Cambridge University Press, 1999, pp. 139–154; and (iii) Leela Kasturi and Vina Mazumdar (eds), *Women and Indian Nationalism*. New Delhi: Vikas Publishing

House, 1994, pp. xxv–xxvii. Kamaladevi Chattopadhyay, *Indian Women's Battle for Freedom*. New Delhi: Abhinav Publications, 1983, provides valuable insights from a first-person vantage. Thapar-Bjorkert (pp. 263–264) while conceding that the participation of women was 'circumscribed by male nationalist leaders, and that women's roles in the family were redefined rather than completely overturned', avers that their attempts to use 'the dominant nationalist ideology to alter their own lives ... did not lead to full emancipation, ... [but] did enable resistance to pre-existing familial structures.'

2. Gyanendra Pandey, *The Ascendancy of the Congress in Uttar Pradesh, 1926–34: A Study in Imperfect Mobilisation*. Delhi: Oxford University Press, 1978. This work has been revised and re-issued in 2002 as *The Ascendancy of the Congress in Uttar Pradesh: Class, Community and Nation in Northern India, 1926–1940*, by Anthem Press, London.
3. Bipan Chandra et al, *India's Struggle for Independence*. New Delhi: Penguin Books, 1989.
4. Visalakshi Menon, *Indian Women and Nationalism – The U.P. Story*. New Delhi: Shakti Books, Har-Anand Publications, 2003.
5. For a re-examination of the matrix of education, social reform and the women's question in late nineteenth century Colonial India, and its imperfections, see Amiya P. Sen, *Social and Religious Reform: The Hindus of British India*, New Delhi: Oxford University Press, 1985, and Kenneth W. Jones, *Socio-Religious Reform Movements in British India*, Cambridge: Cambridge University Press, 1989.
6. Gail Minault, *Secluded Scholars: Women's Education and Muslim Social Reform in Colonial India*. Delhi: Oxford University Press, 1999.
7. V. Menon, *Indian Women and Nationalism*, p. 35.
8. Ibid., p. 37.
9. Madhu Kishwar, 'Arya Samaj and Women's Education, Kanya Mahavidyalya, Jalandhar', Review of Women's Studies, *Economic and Political Weekly*, Vol. XXI, No. 17 (26 April 1986), pp. WS-9–WS-24. The quoted phrases are on pp. WS-12 and WS-18.
10. Ibid., p. WS-19.

11. Ibid., pp. WS-20; WS-19.
12. Quoted in V. Menon, *Indian Women and Nationalism*, p. 40, from David Ruben (trans.), *Widows, Wives and other Heroines – Twelve Stories by Premchand*. Delhi: OUP, 1998, pp. 19–21.
13. V. Menon, *Indian Women and Nationalism*, p. 49.
14. Sumit Sarkar, *Modern India 1885–1947*. New Delhi: MacMillan, 1983, p. 290; Jawaharlal Nehru, *An Autobiography*, New Delhi: Oxford University Press Edition, 1980, p. 300.
15. *Famine Inquiry Commission. Final Report*. Delhi: Manager of Publications, 1945, pp. 276–278.
16. K. Sarədamoni, 'Women and Development', *in* C. Sheshadri and J.L. Pandey (eds), *Population Education: A National Source Book*, Vol. II. New Delhi: NCERT, 1991, p. 142.
17. Sri Narayan Chaturvedi, *The History of Rural Education in the United Provinces of Agra and Oudh (1840–1926)*. Allahabad: The Indian Press, 1930, pp. 145–147. For an informative account of the trends in female literacy – overall, locality-wise and across divergent social groups – in the United Provinces during the period 1901–1931, gleaned mainly from successive Census Reports, see Nirula, *Women Problems and Their Oppression in U.P.* Delhi: APH Publishing Corporation, 2009, pp. 23–51.
18. Shahida Lateef, 'The Indian Women's Movement and National Development: An Overview', in Gail Minault (ed.), *The Extended Family*. Delhi: Chanakya Publications, 1981, p. 199.
19. G. Pandey, *The Ascendancy of the Congress*, p. 27.
20. Sumit Sarkar, *Modern India*, p. 222.
21. Malabika Pande, *Gandhi's Vision of Social Transformation*. Jaipur: Rawat Publications, 2011, pp. 33–36.
22. *Collected Works of Mahatma Gandhi* [CWMG hereinafter], Vol. XIV, p. 61.
23. Ibid., Vol. XV, p. 189.
24. Ibid., p. 441.

25. Ibid., Vol. XXIV, p. 183.
26. R.C. Majumdar (ed.), *Struggle for Freedom* (*Vol. XI: The History and Culture of the Indian People*). Bombay: Bharatiya Vidya Bhawan, 1969, pp. 472–473.
27. J. L. Nehru, *An Autobiography*, pp. 161–62.
28. *The Indian Statutory* [Simon] *Commission*, 1928 as quoted in Pandey, *The Ascendancy of the Congress*, p. 77.
29. *Chaand*, January 1938, p. 318.
30. *Satyagraha Samachar* (issued daily by the Satyagraha Committee of Prayag), edited by Baijnath Kapoor, and printed at the Abhyudaya Press, Allahabad, from April 1930; files available at U.P. State Archives, Lucknow.
31. Recollected during interview with Pratibha Malaviya, daughter of Ketaki Bhatt, Freedom Fighter of Allahabad.

CHAPTER 1

Women, Education and Politics in the United Provinces: An Overview, 1916–1942

This chapter, instead of examining the state of women's education *per se*, proposes to consider whether there was any correlation between the growth of women's education and their political participation in the United Provinces between 1916 and 1942. At the outset, it may be stated that the rate of literacy need not be the most accurate indicator of the growth of education for all classes. Female education was in a deplorable state all over the country; the female literacy rate was 2.9 per cent in 1931[1] and stood at 1.7 per cent in Allahabad in that year.[2] The general colonial attitude towards mass education is well summed up in the celebrated critique of the senior British civil servant, Arthur Mayhew C.I.E., who was Director of Public Instruction, Central Provinces in the early decades of the twentieth century. 'If the Government by their initial exclusion of the masses', he wrote, 'accentuated the segregation of these masses from the privileged few, by their initial restriction of their efforts to the male population they brought a line of division, where it has never existed before, within the household.' Even when the problem of women's education was recognized, he continued, 'no funds were allotted . . . [and] the problem was not seriously considered. The sex which was marked out by nature to be a domestic ornament in England might safely be left to the same function in India. Danger, in fact, lay in any other course.'[3]

In spite of the generally bleak picture of women's education, the United Provinces presented a paradox in terms of women's political mobilization, especially from the second decade of the twentieth century. It was the Partition of Bengal in 1905 and the spontaneous and vigorous anti-Partition or *Swadeshi* movement which followed it, that acted as a big catalyst for the political mobilization of women in Bengal,[4] and beyond as well for the reverberations of the movement were felt in other provinces, notably the Presidencies of Bombay and Madras, the United Provinces, the Central Provinces and the Punjab.[5] Another big contribution of the anti-Partition movement in Bengal was the concept of 'national education', which had for its underlying principle 'love of the motherland'.[6] In accordance with this principle numerous educational institutions were set up which took no aid from the government. Most of these institutions did not strike deep roots at the time, but they did serve a very important purpose – they became role models during the second mass upheaval which followed the entry of Mohandas Karamchand Gandhi into national politics in 1919.

Another factor which played a part in the politicization of women was the 'mediating role of members of the female intelligentsia', who had more time to absorb nationalist ideals, as most of them were not involved in working for a living.[7] Many became leaders in both the women's and the national movements. Important among them were Pandita Ramabai, Sarojini Naidu, Sarala Devi Chaudhurani, Annie Besant and Sister Nivedita. Sarojini Naidu and Annie Besant were particularly active in the United Provinces. Their role is highlighted in Chapters 3 and 4.

The Home Rule Movement of 1916–1917, which was a pioneer in mass movements in the country, was a major contributor towards raising the political consciousness of women in India. Launched under the (initially separate) leadership of Mrs Annie Besant and Bal Gangadhar Tilak, the movement had for its goal self-government within the British Empire by all constitutional means.[8] Along with leading cities in other provinces,[9] four centres of the Home Rule League were set up in the United Provinces, namely at Allahabad, Varanasi, Kanpur and Mathura, which became the foci of public activity.[10] Annie Besant's extensive tours, stirring addresses and powerful writing skills moved the country in a way that had not been achieved before. The two leagues, one of Mrs Besant and the other of Tilak, worked in harmony and were so successful that the Viceroy, Lord Chelmsford, wrote in alarm to the Secretary of State, E.S. Montagu: 'The agitation is having mischievous effect on public feeling throughout the country.'[11] An important characteristic of the movement was the participation of women.[12]

An important outcome of the Home Rule Movement was the election of Annie Besant as the President of the Indian National Congress in 1917, the first time a woman held the office. This particular session in Calcutta was attended by over 400 women apart from 5,000 delegates and an equal number of visitors. Her Presidential Address was symbolic of the new national spirit sweeping across the country. She demanded freedom for India for two reasons: first, because it was the birth right of every nation, and second, because it was the basic principle of national development.[13]

Sociologically speaking, a vital input in the matter of political socialization of an individual is the family background or, more specifically, the political leanings of the family. Ehsanul Haq writes: 'The family is the most important source of political socialization of school boys. The formal system of schooling has a limited role to play. It is a secondary institution which reinforces what the family, the informal and primary institution does.'[14]

Although Haq's study focuses specifically on boys, his conclusions are equally relevant for girls in the Indian context. With the process of maturation, writes Haq, other agencies like the school, the teachers, participation in voluntary associations, peer groups and the mass media become more important.[15]

The point about the political orientation of the family and its importance for political socialization of the children becomes clear when the following facts are considered. Most of the United Provinces was a stronghold of the Indian National Congress, which was the flag-bearer of the nationalist movement in the country. A large number of families in the United Provinces owed political allegiance to the Congress, and, hence, the women were bound to be affected. This is confirmed in the course of interviews with the women activists or people closely associated with them.

Although female education was, as noted above, in an appalling state in the United Provinces generally, two facts must be remembered as they are of considerable relevance to our study; first, it developed quite rapidly in the urban areas, and second, there was noticeable progress from 1917. This was mainly due to private enterprise and the efforts of popular Indian governments under the Dyarchy instituted by the Government of India Act of 1919, although financial stringency was common as central help was not forthcoming. In fact, under the Dyarchy, 'the finances of the Provincial Governments were largely crippled by the contributions payable to the Government of India.'[16] Moreover, the portfolio of finance was a 'reserved' subject held by an executive councillor who generally had no sympathy for a 'transferred' department under an Indian minister. Another important failure under the Dyarchy 'was the sudden cessation of financial assistance from the central government'.[17]

About education being an urban phenomenon, Aparna Basu writes: 'Literacy was much higher in the districts having a small area but containing large cities such as Benares, Allahabad, Lucknow, Agra, than in the province as a whole. Literacy in the United Provinces in 1921 was 65 per 1000 males, while in the 24 cities it was 213 per 1000. Benares came first with 289, Allahabad had 287, Gorakhpur 270 and so on.'[18]

The somewhat parallel development of national consciousness and female education in the United Provinces becomes evident when the figures for primary education are compared in the years 1917 and 1920. According to the *General Report on Public Instruction in the United Provinces of Agra and Oudh for 1917*[19] there were 1,083 girls' primary schools with 36,426 pupils, while the Report of 1920 mentions 1,222 girls' primary schools with 41,624 pupils. Moreover, the Report of 1917 bears no reference to collegiate education of girls while that of 1920 mentions the Isabella Thoburn College in Lucknow where both Intermediate and BA classes were held for girls. Meanwhile, the independent Jagat Taran Girl's School which had opened in Allahabad for Bengali girls had also begun Intermediate classes. Intermediate classes began in 1921 at three more centres, the Theosophical College, Banaras, Muslim High School, Lucknow and Muhammadan Anglo-Oriental Girls School, Aligarh.[20]

The *Quinquennial Report* of 1922 records substantial progress at almost every level of female education and notes, 'it is possible that the ferment of politics has created a desire for more knowledge among women.' The total enrolment of Indian girls increased by 21 per cent from 1917. As compared to 49,955 female students in 1916–1917 there were 60,711 female students in 1921–1922, with a preponderance in lower primary classes. Growth of collegiate education was the 'most marked feature of quinquennium'. Intermediate classes opened at two more centres, Mahadevi Kanya Pathshala in Dehradun and Mahila Vidyalaya, Lucknow. Anglo-vernacular secondary schools, especially in the middle classes, showed a 23 per cent increase in enrolment: there were 966 pupils in 1916–1917, as against 1,239 in 1921–1922. Vernacular middle schools showed a very small increase, but enrolment in primary schools rose from 1,083 pupils in 1917 to 1,337 in 1922. The average number of pupils in them rose from 33,398 to

42,129. District Board schools recorded an increase of 55 per cent in the number of scholars. However, the Report observed that this would have been much higher had there been more funds available to start more schools and to improve the position of staff and equipment in existing schools. Another positive feature was an 88 per cent increase in spending on education, as the total expenditure for 1921–1922 was Rs. 1,101,082 as against Rs. 584,493 in 1916–1917. Of the total increase of Rs. 516,589 the share from provincial funds was Rs. 274,345. The share of municipal funds also increased, signifying a growing interest in female education in towns.[21]

The *Quinquennial Report* of 1927[22] shows progressive increase in the number of institutions of all kinds for Indian girls as well as in the number of girls enrolled in those institutions. As regards the relative progress of different communities in public instruction there was a steady increase in the number of Indian Christians (from 1,080 to 4,437) and high-caste Hindus (from 44,527 to 57,110), but remarkable progress could be seen in the number of girls from depressed classes (464 to 2,221) and the Muslim community (8,266 to 12,643). Anglo-vernacular high schools and middle schools recorded an increase of 73 per cent in enrolment, from 1,239 in 1922 to 2,145 in 1927, and this trend was mainly seen in relation to Indian Christians and Hindu girls. Out of 361 pupils who appeared for the Anglo-vernacular middle examination, 251 passed. The number of vernacular middle schools increased by almost 50 per cent in the quinquennium, from 79 in 1922 to 153 in 1927, but the Report admitted that they were in a bad shape in rural areas due to paucity of teachers. Primary schools, especially those managed by District Boards, showed considerable increase due to larger grants. Municipal schools had also progressed but not to the extent witnessed in the preceding quinquennium. Girls studying in boys' primary schools was a common phenomenon; in 1926–1927 there were 39,200 girls who studied in boys' primary schools, which constituted 31.55 per cent of total enrolment. These schools were mostly of the preparatory kind, and girls up to the age of 10 years were allowed to study in them.

The correlation between the national movement for freedom and the spread of female education is evident from the unprecedented progress recorded in the ensuing quinquennium (1927–1932). The section on *The Education of Girls* (Chapter 7) in the *(Quinquennial) General Report on Public Instruction 1927–1932* had this to say: 'The encouraging feature of the quinquennium is that public opinion in regard to girls education has changed and in many places and among many communities indifference has been succeeded by appreciation. This is manifested by (1) a willingness to prolong the school life of girls, (2) an active desire to raise the standard of education and (3) a demand for additional schools. It is to be regretted that at this juncture progress should be hampered by the lack of funds.'[23] Even the Report of the Hartog Committee (1929), that is, the *Auxiliary Committee on Educational Development* under the Simon Commission, remarked: 'Education has come to be regarded generally as a matter of primary national importance, an indispensable agency in the difficult task of nation building.' It further stated that sections which had till then kept away from education due to social prejudice came forward in large numbers – women, Muhammedans, depressed classes and tribal aborigines.'[24]

The total number of recognized educational institutions for girls went up from 1,807 in 1927 to 2,021 in 1932, an increase of 11 per cent, while enrolment jumped up by 30.7 per cent, from 78,080 to 102,058. Even the number of unrecognized educational institutions rose sharply by 24 per cent in the period, from 177 to 220, with enrolment rising by 19 per cent, from 3,205 to 3,802. The number of girls reading in boys schools in 1932 was 57,000, up from the corresponding figure of 39,200 for the preceding quinquennium. The enhancement in the enrolment of pupils in various stages of instruction during the quinquennium 1927–1932 is a revelation. The rise was 40 per cent (from 253 to 335) at the high school stage and of a remarkable quantum of

125 per cent (from 1,992 to 4,474) at the middle school stage, and stood at a respectable 74 per cent (from 5,398 to 9,390) at the upper primary level. The increments were at 45 per cent (from 17,817 to 25,768) for the lower primary and, disappointingly, at a mere 18 per cent (from 57,815 to 61,220) for the preparatory stage. Thus, the greatest increase was at the secondary stage. The community-wise enumeration of progress in female education revealed an increase of 11 per cent among Indian Christians, 32 per cent among high-caste Hindus, 25 per cent among depressed-class Hindus and 34 per cent among Muhammedans.

Total direct expenditure on girl's education rose in the quinquennium from Rs. 1,442,183 (in 1927) to Rs. 1,928,697 in 1932. Of this the largest contribution was from provincial revenues, which rose from Rs. 688,351 (1927) to Rs. 974,340 in 1932. The provincial revenues were spent on (1) normal schools and training classes, (2) government vernacular schools in districts and (3) grants to aided schools. Revenues from fees almost doubled, from Rs. 53,674 to Rs. 149,781 in the quinquennium.

As far as Anglo-vernacular education was concerned, the position of university education remained as before during the quinquennium, but enrolment in intermediate classes rose from 87 to 125 while that at the secondary stage enrolment rose from 2,145 in 1927 to 4,809 in 1932. The number of high schools increased from 11 to 13. Even vernacular education registered a good deal of progress. The number of candidates for the vernacular lower middle examination (Class VI) rose from 540 in 1927 to 1,418 in 1932, which included 869 school candidates while 549 were private candidates. This showed that many more pupils were now studying beyond the primary stage. The number of vernacular middle schools increased from 153 to 186 in 1932. Their distribution was as follows: 70 were aided schools, 65 government, 26 municipal board, 23 district board and 2 were unaided.

In the sphere of primary education, the number of schools rose from 1,568 in 1927 to 1,719 in 1932 and the number of students increased from 54,118 to 64,291. Average attendance in schools providing primary education increased from 39,413 to 47,122. The Report noted that during this period (1927–1932) apathy had been replaced by interest, but primary education continued to suffer due to paucity of funds and competent teaching staff, which really was its consequence.

Except for the English Teacher's Certificate examination, there was a sharp increase in the number of candidates for the various Teachers' Certificate examinations. For the vernacular lower-middle examination the number of students who cleared the examination rose from 615 to 1,541; for the Anglo-vernacular middle examination the increase was from 366 to 714, while for the Vernacular Teachers Certificate examination the number rose from 94 to 120 in 1932. The decline was only for the English Teacher's Certificate, which fell from 27 to 18.

The steady progress discernible in the United Provinces at the secondary and middle stages of girls' education continued apace in the quinquennium 1932–1937.[25] Although the total number of recognized educational institutions for girls increased only by 8 per cent, from 2,021 to 2,184, and enrolment by 33 per cent, from 135,564 to 335,006, the number of girls studying in boys' schools increased by almost 50 per cent, from 57,000 in 1932 to 85,565 in 1937, which showed that there was less *purdah* or social prejudice then, and this increase was most seen in primary schools. The increase in the percentage of girl students in various stages of instruction during the quinquennium was as follows: college – 120 per cent (from 172 in 1932 to 379 in 1937); high school – 146 per cent (from 335 to 823); middle section – 104 per cent (from 4,474 to 9,154); upper primary – 71 per cent (from 9,390 to 16,117); lower primary – 34 per cent (from 25,768 to 34,697); and preparatory section – 20 per cent (from 61,220 to 73,612).

There was also a substantial increase in total expenditure in the quinquennium. It rose from Rs. 1,928,697 in 1932 to Rs. 2,578,327. As before, the major part of this amount was a contribution from provincial revenues, at Rs. 1,278,899. Municipal Board funds constituted Rs. 442,731, and fees collected amounted to Rs. 295,131; there was a decrease in District Board funds; other sources contributed Rs. 408,673.

As far as university education of girls was concerned, the Isabella Thoburn College in Lucknow was the only one of its kind in the United Provinces, but women's hostels were attached to the Universities of Allahabad and Lucknow and to the Benares Hindu University, along with separate classes for undergraduate girls. College education also made progress, as the number of intermediate colleges for girls rose to eight. However, the greatest expansion during the quinquennium was in secondary education: the enrolment of girls rose from 4,809 in 1932 to 9,977 in 1937; the number of high schools admitting girls increased from 13 to 19. Nine new high schools for girls were opened in the period, as follows:

1. Jubilee High School (for Bengali girls), Lucknow
2. Arya Kanya Pathshala, Allahabad
3. Muhammedan Girls Jubilee High School, Moradabad
4. Morari Lal Khatri High School, Agra
5. Raghunath Girls High School, Meerut
6. Arya Kanya Pathshala High School, Bahadurganj, Shahjahanpur
7. Balrampur Girls High School, Balrampur
8. Hewett Model Girls High School, Muzzafarnagar
9. Government Girls High School, Bareilly.

As a consequence of the national awakening, extensive official and nonofficial efforts were made in this period to spread higher education among women and the less advanced classes of the population. The driving initiatives may be categorized as follows:

(1) Government attempts at opening special institutions with reserved accommodation for different sections, awards of scholarships, free studentships and provision of preferential recruitment in government services, etc.

(2) Attempts made by communities themselves to organize funds for scholarships, hostels, etc.

(3) Attempts by philanthropic social service organizations.

A point to be noted is that most of this expansion at the secondary stage was due to private enterprise,[26] a reflection of the nationalist spirit.

English middle schools for girls increased in number from 47 to 64, and the number of pupils rose from 4,474 to 9,542. This expansion was due to the fact that many of these schools began admitting Hindu girls and Hindi became the first vernacular to be taught. An example was the Adams Girls School in Almora, where 47 per cent of the girls were Hindu.[27] Girls vernacular middle schools of all kinds also increased in number, from 186 in 1932 to 249 in 1937, while their enrolment rose from 26,219 pupils in 1932 to 38,896 in 1937.

Girls vernacular primary schools, except those of the government and district board, recorded progress. They increased in number from 1,719 in 1932 to 1,785 in 1937, and enrolment increased from 64,246 in 1932 to 78,860 in 1937. Government policy was not to open more primary schools for girls in rural areas where female education was almost entirely primary, but to develop existing schools as spread of coeducation was progressing in villages. However, coeducation was not common in urban areas; hence, more girls' primary schools were opened there. As compared to the substantial advance in higher and middle stages, there was 'little progress' in the primary sector due to financial stringency caused by the world economic depression. Government contributions were, in consequence, smaller than that of nongovernment sources. According to Syed Nurullah and J.P. Naik, 'no serious attempts were made either to introduce compulsion extensively or to enforce it rigidly.'[28] The position in this regard in the United Provinces was as follows in 1936–1937:

	Urban areas	Rural areas	Number of villages
United Provinces	36	25	1224

Although compulsion was more needed for girls, it was not applied.

The overall position of female education was indeed sorry. According to the *General Report on Public Instruction* for the Quinquennium 1932–1937, 'only one in every eight girls reaches middle stage and that too in big towns... 88 per cent of girls entering schools do not attain literacy.' Progress in the following quinquennium (1937–1942)[29] was checked to a considerable extent due to the economic situation created by the Second World War which hit hard the urban middle class.[30] However, university and college education expanded for several reasons, such as the general awakening due to the war and the national movement, the expansion of secondary education in the previous quinquennium and the desire for higher education that was quickly spreading among women and backward classes.[31] Apart from the women's colleges attached to the Universities of Lucknow, Benares, Allahabad, Agra and Aligarh another women's college named Mahila Vidyalaya was affiliated to the Lucknow University. The number of intermediate colleges rose from 8 to 11 with a total enrolment of 4,461, but none of these colleges were of the government.[32] The number of high schools increased from 19 to 40, and their enrolment figure was 14,618 in 1941–1942. Vernacular middle schools increased from 249 in 1937 to 352 in 1942. The number of vernacular primary schools actually decreased from 1,785 to 1,605 for reasons stated earlier.

If the total population of females in the United Provinces in 1941–1942 is considered (26,167,400) and further that of girls between the age of 6 and 11 (3,130,248) then it will be seen that only 5.7 per cent of these, that is, 179,258, were attending primary schools. This shows how much remained to be done before the female population could be made literate.

However, what is relevant for our study is that there was a progressive increase right through the period in the number of girls in the middle and higher classes in the urban areas, and, as stated earlier, there was stark contrast between the literacy rates of the urban and rural areas. This supports our contention that the highest level of political mobilization of women was in urban areas during the period of this study. Recent research has shown that peasant women from Pratapgarh, some on their own initiative, offered themselves for arrest during the individual satyagraha campaign. But that is another story![33]

NOTES

1. K. Saradamoni, 'Women and Development', in C. Sheshadri and J.L. Pandey (eds), *Population Education: A National Source Book*, Vol. 2. New Delhi: NCERT, 1991, p. 142.
2. *Uttar Pradesh District Gazetteers*: *Allahabad*. Government of Uttar Pradesh, Lucknow, 1966, p. 266.
3. Arthur Mayhew, *The Education of India: A Study of British Educational Policy in India 1835–1920 and of its Bearing on National Life and Problems in India Today*. London: Faber and Gwyer Limited, 1926, pp. 96, 97.
4. Leela Kasturi and Vina Mazumdar, 'Women and Indian Nationalism'. Occasional Paper No. 20, 1994. New Delhi: Centre for Women's Development Studies, p. 14.
5. R.C. Majumdar (ed.), *Struggle for Freedom* (Vol. 11 of *The History and Culture of the Indian People)*. Bombay: Bharatiya Vidya Bhawan, 1969, p. 45.

6. Syed Nurullah and J.P. Naik, *A Students' History of Education in India, 1800–1947*. Bombay: Macmillan and Co., 1951, pp. 261–265.
7. Kasturi and Mazumdar, 'Women and Indian Nationalism', p. 16.
8. R.C. Majumdar, *Struggle for Freedom*, p. 251.
9. Notably, Bombay, Calicut, Madras and Ahmadnagar, in the first instance.
10. R.C. Majumdar, *Struggle for Freedom*, p. 250.
11. Ibid., p. 255.
12. Ibid., p. 253.
13. Ibid., p. 257
14. Ehsanul Haq, *Education and Political Culture in India: The Limits of Schooling System and Political Socialisation*. New Delhi: Sterling Publishers, 1981. Preface, p. xiii.
15. Ibid., pp. 13–18.
16. S. Nurullah and J.P. Naik, *A Students' History of Education in India*, p. 277.
17. Ibid., p. 279.
18. Aparna Basu, *The Growth of Education and Political Development in India, 1898–1920*, Delhi: Oxford University Press, 1974, p. 141.
19. *General Report on Public Instruction in the United Provinces of Agra and Oudh 1917*, Chapter 7, UP State Archives, Lucknow.
20. *General Report on Public Instruction 1921*, UP State Archives, Lucknow.
21. *Quinquennial Report on Public Instruction in the United Provinces of Agra and Oudh* [*QRPI* hereinafter], 1922, Chapter 7, UP State Archives, Lucknow.
22. *QRPI*, 1927.
23. *QRPI*, 1932.
24. S. Nurullah and J.P. Naik, *A Students' History of Education in India*, pp. 283–284. The Auxiliary Committee of Sir Philip Hartog was asked to review the growth of education in British India.

25. *QRPI*, 1937.
26. S. Nurullah and J.P. Naik, *A Students' History of Education in India*, pp. 295.
27. *QRPI*, 1937.
28. S. Nurullah and J.P. Naik, *A Students' History of Education in India*, pp. 308.
29. *QRPI*, 1942.
30. Ibid., 326.
31. Ibid., 322.
32. *QRPI*, 1942.
33. Kapil Kumar, 'Rural Women in Awadh, 1917–1947: Baba Ram Chandra and the Women's Question', in Kumkum Sangari and Sudesh Vaid (eds), *Recasting Women: Essays in Colonial History*. New Delhi: Kali for Women, 1989, pp. 337–369 and 365–367.

CHAPTER 2

National Education and Its Impact

The nationalist perspective on education was indeed quite different (though internally varied) from the colonial system of education, which may be 'viewed as a means of the prosecution and reproduction of colonial authority, not only "cognitive" authority but also "political" authority, among the "natives" of the colonized country'.[1] Another dimension of the educational scene in the colonial period was the preservation of traditional social hierarchy of underprivileged castes and denial of educational equity to them and other tribal groups.[2] A major contributor to this pattern, believe Joseph Bara and Krishna Kumar, was the Indian middle class which had firmly entrenched itself into the bureaucracy and the social system in general and it could not compromise with any educational measure that it feared could destabilize their established social position.[3]

The nationalist position on British educational policy was that by imposing the use of English as the medium of higher education, cultural as well as political domination was secured. The technical problems in transferring modern knowledge to the Indian languages were seen as substantial though in principle negotiable.

A problem that was recognized was that the multiplicity of major languages in the country would pose problems in the adoption of any one language as the national language.[4] The need for technical and vocational education for the nation's progress was another major consideration, particularly since the defeat of Russia by Japan in 1905. It was believed that Japan's technical prowess based on education and training network was responsible for her success. This led to the setting up of the Bengal National Council of Technical Education in 1906 in Calcutta and development of engineering, mining and metallurgy education at Banaras Hindu University in 1916–1917.[5] High-level scientific research was also sought to be propagated by nationalist educationists like Gurudas Banerji and Ashutosh Mukherjee through the Calcutta University and affiliated colleges in Calcutta in early twentieth century.

A major advance and a different direction in the national perspective on education came after the radical change in the national political movement under the leadership of Gandhi in the 1920s. He was not opposed to higher scientific education and research which he thought could be better cared for by private enterprise; his sole concentration was on mass education with a vision of a Sarvodaya Society. The basic elements in it were self-sufficiency, self-reliance, use of the mother tongue and liberation of the child from the tyranny of text books, rote memory and examinations.[6] Humanistic educators like Zakir Hussain and K.G. Saiyidain were foremost in concretizing Gandhi's scheme of Basic Education, better known as the Wardha Scheme or Nai Talim.

It is now proposed to briefly trace the developmental history of national education in India as it will provide the necessary backdrop to our main theme – *education* and *political mobilization of women* in the pre-Independence period. Aparna Basu argues that the idea of nationalism and national education arose in France after the French Revolution. It was said that to promote national unity all children should have a uniform system of education which required centralized control. In Prussia, and later in a United Germany under Bismarck, education was used to foster loyalty to the state, a trend which reached its apogee in Nazi Germany, Fascist Italy, the erstwhile Soviet Union and Japan before the Second World War.[7]

National education in India arose not to promote loyalty to the British rulers but to oppose their educational system, which according to them was the root of British hegemony. It was believed that the British system denationalized the youth and produced only clerks and lawyers. In the last decades of the nineteenth century, a number of educational movements were started to replace the existing system. Indian culture, interpreted variously as Hindu or Muslim, came to form the basis of one school of thought. The Arya Samaj opened the Dayanand Anglo-Vedic (DAV) schools and colleges and the *gurukul* at Kangri where apart from modern subjects the emphasis was on Sanskrit and Hindu learning, particularly in the *gurukul*. The Central Hindu College started by Annie Besant in Varanasi also stressed India's ancient heritage and the study of Hinduism. The seminary at Deoband in the United Provinces imparted Islamic learning, while the Khalsa colleges in Punjab taught the tenets of Sikhism.

Another important experiment was made in Maharashtra, where Vishnu Shastri Chiplunkar started the New English School. He was joined by four young nationalists, all graduates of Bombay University, namely Bal Gangadhar Tilak, *Gopal Ganesh Agarkar,* V.B. Karandikar and Mahadeo Ballal Namjoshi. Together they also founded the Deccan Education Society (DES) in 1884 with the goal of a new kind of education which would restore the self-respect of the country. Gopal Krishna Gokhale became an ardent supporter of the DES. Lacking in resources, their efforts required government patronage and support; hence, the college of DES was named after the retiring governor of Bombay, Sir James Fergusson. What distinguished the DES in its early years was the spirit of self-sacrifice and dedication of its life members, directors and teachers.[8] To make their education as accessible as possible, fees were low, teachers accepted minimum salaries and soon the Fergusson College acquired a good reputation.

The catalyst for nationalist effort in the field of education in Bengal was Curzon's University reforms which were criticized as an attempt to place education under government control. As the proposed Universities Bill required stricter conditions of affiliation of colleges, higher fees and so on, it was feared that the government aimed to restrict the spread of higher education. In protest, the editor of *Dawn*, Satish Chandra Mukherjee, founded the Dawn Society in July 1902. Radical efforts had begun with the beginning of the *Swadeshi* campaign in 1901–1902, much before the actual partition of Bengal in 1905. Most of the participants were students and members of the intelligentsia, many of them journalists who picketed shops selling foreign cloth, organized political meetings, staged demonstrations and propagated *swadeshi*. Their slogan was the famous *Vande Mataram* from Bankim Chandra Chatterjee's revolutionary novel *Anandamath*.

It was the 'Carlyle Circular'[9] which aimed at stamping out the participation of students and colleges in the *swadeshi* movement that led to the next stage in the growth of national education. Leaders of the anti-partition movement such as Bipin Chandra Pal and Surendranath Banerjee held meetings and wrote articles on establishing a National University.[10] The first national school was started in Rangpur district in East Bengal in 1905. This became the pattern for other national schools in Dacca, Dinajpur and Mymensingh. Many declared themselves national after the withdrawal of government grants. In 1907 there was just one secondary-level national school, but by 1909 there were approximately 40 national schools in the two Bengals. There were also a few girls' schools, for example, those at Mymensingh and Naogaon (Rajshahi).[11]

Finally, a manifesto issued by Asutosh Choudhury called for the boycott of Calcutta University, which was followed by a meeting of leading public men of the city at the Bengal landholders association under the Presidency of Raja Ram Mohan Mukherjee. Here the National Council of Education (NCE) was established with the object of imparting education, literary as well as scientific and technical on national lines and exclusively under national control, not in opposition to, but standing apart from the existing systems of primary, secondary and university education. Among the aims were some unique features like providing for denominational religious education, inspiring patriotism and national service, and encouragement of indigenous learning like *Ayurvedic* and *Hakimi* systems in medical education.

Another section of the intelligentsia headed by Tarak Nath Palit started the Society for the Promotion of Technical Education, which set up the Bengal Technical Institute in July 1906. The NCE also organized a system of grants-in-aid, scholarships and stipends. Initially money came from *zamindars* (landlords) like Subodh Chandra Mullick and the rajas of Gourpur and Mymensingh; nevertheless, local organizations like Swadesh Bandhab Samiti of Bakarganj or the Sebak Samiti of Comicha also chipped in. Financial help was also given by local zamindars, pleaders and *Mukhtars.* Teachers had to take the vow of *Swadeshi* before receiving a grant. Funds were also raised by teachers and pupils through theatrical performances held at river *ghats* and railway stations and by other means.'[12]

The national schools in Bengal became centres of political activity and were also used as rendezvous points by political extremists. Many were closely linked with secret revolutionary societies such as the *Anusilan Samiti* of Dacca and the *Swadesh Bandhab Samiti* of Bakarganj. The pattern of political teaching consisted of singing patriotic songs (composed in profusion at this time), poems, lathi drills, and the reading and distribution of anti-government newspapers and literature.

The 1905–1908 Swadeshi movement in Bengal reflects the beginning of women's participation in nationalist activities on a larger scale. From August 1905, the participation of women was reported; 500 women watched the laying of the foundation stone of the Federation Hall in Calcutta on August 24; on the same day, Ranendra Sundar Trivedis' *Banglalakhir Brata Katha* (the Story of the Bengali Women's Vow) was read before a women's meeting in his village in Murshidabad district. The *Brata Katha* intended to translate the Swadeshi message for village women; it urged them to foster Hindu–Muslim unity and above all to take a vow to abstain from foreign cloth. It was hoped that Lakshmi, the goddess of fortune, would reign forever in the golden fields of Bengal.[13]

In the initial stage, many of the wives, sisters and daughters of nationalists had begun to form support groups for the movement. Gradually nationalist women from the middle class contributed jewellery as well as money to Swadeshi; there is a report that in some villages women began to put aside a handful of grain as contribution, and in Barisal, many women made over their savings to Ashwin Kumar Dutta's *Swadesh Bandhab Samiti*. In Khulna, women smashed their foreign bangles after a speech given by Kaliprasanna Kabvanisnarod; when B.C. Pal toured Bengal in 1907, he addressed women's meetings in Habibganj and Bhola, and when Surendra Nath Banerjee visited Mymensingh in the same year, he was given a rousing welcome by women.[14] In August 1907, when Bhupendranath Datta (Swami Vivekananda's brother) was arrested, a Ladies Meeting was held in his support, an address of honour was signed by 200 women and presented to his mother, and contributions were made for his legal expenses.[15] Sister Nivedita, one of Vivekananda's most ardent disciples, stood surety for Bhupendra Nath.[16]

In Poona, Maharashtra, a meeting of about 'a hundred and twenty high caste Brahmin ladies' was reported in support of the Swadeshi movement on 6 October 1905. They assembled on a religious occasion, presided over by Parwati Bapat, where essays on the 'Swadeshi Question' were read by Saraswati Bhanu and Miss Bhatkande, and all resolved that they would not buy glass bangles, children's toys or any other items manufactured in Europe.[17]

Punjab already had a record of active propagation of Swadeshi by the Arya Samaj from the 1880s, but women appeared to have joined the movement around the same time as that in Bengal. During the 1905 Swadeshi movement, *Panchal Pandita* (magazine of Kanya Mahavidyalaya, Jalandhar) was in the forefront of propaganda; its publications and articles urged women to recognize that with their involvement Swadeshi would spread much faster. The January 1906 issue of *Panchal Pandita* carried a lengthy article on how imported goods had destroyed local industry and drained the country of its wealth.[18] *Ved Prachar* gave way to nationalist propaganda, and Vande Matram became the prayer appearing in the magazine. Students were urged to plan for the uplift of both the nation and Indian women.[19]

The Industrial and Agricultural Exhibition at Lahore in 1909 had a Ladies section organized by them. Sushila Debi in Sialkot exhorted women to join the movement, organized Swadeshi women's meetings and collected funds for 'anarchists' under trial; Purani, a woman member of the Hissar Arya Samaj, toured several districts of the Punjab, exhorting women to bring up their sons not with a view to join government service but for independent participation in trade, especially the manufacture and sale of Swadeshi goods. She further advocated that they should also be trained to become warriors and great men.[20]

From the foregoing it becomes evident that the demand for national education was not confined to Bengal. At the Indian National Congress session in Bengal in 1916, a resolution moved by Hirendra Nath Dutta, Secretary of the NCE, was adopted unanimously. It said that in the opinion of the Congress, 'the time had arrived for people all over the country earnestly to take up the question of national education for both boys and girls, and organize a system of education, literary, scientific and technical, suited to the requirements of the country, on national lines and under national control'. Tilak and Lajpat Rai were enthusiastic advocates of national education.

As political passions subsided with the reversal of the partition of Bengal in 1911, so did the enthusiasm for national education. In any case it was very difficult for educational institutions that were anti-establishment to flourish under the colonial rule. Private education of the nationalist kind survived only at apolitical institutions such as the gurukuls, *Viswabharati*, *Dakshinasti* and the theosophical schools at Adyar and Benaras.[21] The next phase of national education, which was a much more radical one, began under the guidance of Mahatma Gandhi who assumed leadership of the national movement from 1919.

The turning point came with the Jallianwala Bagh massacre of 13 April 1919, the 'cause' of the *Khilafat* and finally the report of the Hunter Committee, which exonerated the architect of the massacre General Dyer that transformed Gandhi from an arch loyalist of the British empire to a confirmed non-cooperator. Gandhi believed that Indians must resolve to give up what he called their 'three infatuations': (a) government schools, (b) law courts and (c) legislatures.[22] He argued that non-cooperation meant refusal to do anything which would enable the government administration to continue to run. That meant a refusal to obey law or pay taxes, take employment under the government, whether in the civil or military sphere, accept titles or honorary positions, boycott the courts and the legislatures, and withdraw children from schools and colleges run or aided by the government. According to Gandhi, only this kind of total non-cooperation would work. It was such a drastic programme of action that to implement it in full would have been extraordinary.[23] Nevertheless, when the Indian National Congress held a special meeting on September 1920, at Calcutta, Gandhi's line of non-cooperation was accepted. This was confirmed at the regular session at Nagpur three months later.

For the first time the national movement assumed a mass character with widespread political awakening in the countryside. Boycott of government educational institutions was according to Gandhi a key factor in the Non-cooperation Movement, and he believed that the earlier Swadeshi movement in Bengal had lesser impact because (a) the students had not been withdrawn from classes and (b) the leaders continued to send their children to colleges. This was 'sinful' in his opinion. 'In my view', he said the 'most important education is to learn to be a man. Submission to slavery is not being a man.'[24] Attending government schools and colleges obviously comprised such slavery.

In the opinion of J.P. Naik in his *History of Education in India*, no other item of boycott had so much success as the boycott of schools and colleges, though statistically, there was no spectacular decline in the number of students during those years.[25] B.R. Nanda has analysed data and found that the number of students in the arts colleges fell by about 4,000 between the academic years 1919–1920 and 1920–1921. In the subsequent academic year, 1921–1922, there was a further fall of 3,000. Similarly at the secondary level, the numbers fell by 30,000 in the first year and another 1,000 or so in the following year. In the place of government schools and colleges 'national' educational institutions were established, and as many as 80,000 students enrolled in them. There were more than 1,200 such institutions.[26] They were established in all kinds of places and at different levels.

Not all Indian leaders agreed with Gandhi's approach; one of the sceptics was Madan Mohan Malaviya, who had recently founded the Banaras Hindu University; he did not want his fledgling institution to be hurt in any way. It was in these circumstances that, at the initiative of Dr Bhagwan Das, an eminent scholar, the Kashi Vidyapith was established in 1921. From the very large number of institutions established at that time, this and the Gujarat Vidyapith are the only ones that have survived successfully till date.[27] The reason for the decline of the other institutions founded in 1921–1922 has been analysed by Amrik Singh and B.R. Nanda and they have concluded that it was the unwillingness of the middle class to sacrifice for the nationalist causes and their non-committal attitude towards India's freedom that led to this decline in the number of *swadeshi* institutions. B.R. Nanda's comment is most telling: 'Gandhi's ultimate aim was the politicization of the masses, but the programme he placed before the country in 1920 largely depended for its success on the responsibilities of the middle class.'[28]

The national movement, particularly the *Khilafat* component, had considerable impact on the politics of education in Aligarh, particularly the Mohammadan Anglo-Oriental School and then the Mohammadan Anglo-Oriental (MAO) College. Both these institutions had been fervently pro-British; both were headed by Englishmen till 1920. Ever since Turkey's defeat became imminent during the First World War, a section of the intelligentsia here became clearly hostile to the colonial government. Maulana Mohammad Ali was the most prominent in this group.

On 20 November 1917, Gandhi paid a visit to Aligarh. The students were so excited by this visit that they unhorsed the carriage in which he was riding and hauled it through the streets themselves. The British principal did not allow a meeting in the Union room but a meeting was nevertheless held elsewhere.[29] Gandhi visited Aligarh again in the company of the Ali brothers on 11 October 1920. The general sentiment was that the college should sever its connection with the government, that is, its continued affiliation with Allahabad University. The students gave a fortnight's ultimatum to the college to this effect and stopped attending classes. The authorities, however, vetoed this step, and parents were asked to recall their children. It was Zakir Hussain who led the agitation. He was on the staff of MAO College, and when he was accused of hypocrisy at a public meeting he resigned his job on the spot.[30]

The MAO College had a long-cherished dream to be granted university status, and it was on this issue that the authorities finally took steps to forcibly evict Mohammad Ali from the premises he had occupied. It was not only Mohammad Ali who walked out, some 225 students walked out with him as well. Two buildings had been rented in advance, and a new campus was set up. This is how Jamia Millia Islamia was established on 29 October 1920. It was an act of faith by a whole new generation of students in 'a bastion of conservatism', for which there were very few parallels during the Non-Cooperation Movement.[31] Hakim Ajmal Khan, well-known nationalist and educationist, moved Jamia

Millia to Delhi and became its first chancellor. After his death in 1927, Dr M.A. Ansari continued to guide and support it. By this time Zakir Hussain and some of his colleagues like Mohammad Mujeeb and Abid Hussain had joined Jamia. This nationalist and intellectual ferment in the Muslim intelligentsia was no doubt responsible for the political mobilization of Muslim women in the radical phase of the national movement which shall be discussed in Chapters 4 and 7.

While discussing the issue of national education it is essential to focus on Gandhi's scheme of Basic Education also known as the Wardha Scheme or *Nai Taleem.* This had evolved from Gandhi's earliest educational efforts made in South Africa during the course of his struggle against the apartheid regime between 1904 and 1911.[32] At the core of this scheme was training in a vocation which would involve both manual and intellectual labour that would in turn enable the child, girl or boy, to earn his or her livelihood. The aim was teaching self-reliance and self-sufficiency, keeping in mind the colonial dependence and subordination of India. Before elaborating further it would be appropriate to keep in mind Joseph Bara's statement that '[b]y the time of the Wardha Scheme, the colonial system had irreparably distorted the popular mind. Education and manual labour came to be considered opposites, and any new experiment was judged in terms of its expediency in leading to a white collar job in town.'[33] Nevertheless, the scheme, with all its flaws, aimed at 'a silent social revolution, fraught with the most far-reaching consequences', to use the words of Gandhi.[34]

Gandhi gave cogent reasons for discarding the colonial pattern of education. First, it did not meet the requirements of the country; secondly, the English language, which was the medium of instruction at the higher level, had created a permanent bar between the highly educated few and the uneducated many. This had prevented knowledge from percolating to the masses and cast '... a burden which has maimed them mentally and made them strangers in their own land'.[35]

Another challenge to the spread of education was the lack of adequate funds. This was one of the primary motives for devising the scheme of Basic Education. Explaining its underlying principle, Gandhi said:

> Taken as a whole, a vocation or vocations are the best medium for the all round development of a boy and girl and, therefore, the syllabus should be woven around vocational training; primary education thus conceived as a whole is bound to be self-supporting, even though for the first or even the second years' course, it may not be wholly so.[36]

He explained that every handicraft had to be taught not merely mechanically, but scientifically so that, the child would know the why and wherefore of every process.

Gandhi's replacement of the colonial system of education by his Wardha scheme was a part of his total philosophy for the uplift of his people. It was a philosophy for political emancipation, social justice, economic progress, communal harmony and religious tolerance through truth, peace and nonviolence.[37] The tradition of political mobilization of students begun in the Swadeshi Movement during 1905–1907 was carried forward by Gandhi on a massive scale. He felt that students and teachers should not keep themselves aloof from politics or the struggle for India's independence. Their participation was imperative as a moral and social obligation because politics encircled all like the coils of a snake and therefore one had to wrestle with it.[38]

Women's education *vis-à-vis* women's participation in the nationalist movement

Although the *swadeshi* movement did focus on the issue of 'national education' it was repeatedly criticized for its neglect of women and mass education.[39] The women's education movement was soon given a new fillip by the entry of nationalist women; they, in turn, redefined the rationale for women's education.

Annie Besant, B.P. Wadia (seated) and G.S. Arundale (standing)

Mahatma Gandhi and Sarojini Naidu at Dandi, April 5, 1930

From its inception, the movement had concentrated on educating women to fulfil their roles as wives and mothers. Annie Besant, in 1904, gave a graphic account of her perception of women's education: 'The national movement for girls' education must be on national lines, it must accept the general Hindu conceptions of women's place in the national life... India needs nobly trained wives and mothers, wise and tender rulers of the household, educated teachers of the young, helpful counsellors of their husbands, skilled nurses of the sick, rather than girl graduates.'[40]

The scope of education was greatly enlarged by Sarojini Naidu when she spoke to the Indian Social Conference at Calcutta in 1906. Describing education as a 'birthright' and comparing it to 'God's pure air which nourishes (man's) body', she said, 'Educate your women and the nation will take care of itself, for it is as true today as it was yesterday and will be to the end of human life that the hand that rocks the cradle rules the world.'[41] This theme was repeated by Madame Cama in 1910, at a meeting of the Egyptian National Congress: 'remember that the hand that rules the cradle is the hand that moulds the character. That soft hand is the chief factor of national life.'[42] By 1917, women like Sarojini Naidu were conceptualizing a public and nationalist role for women. At the Calcutta Congress of 1917 she spoke on the subject of women's political activism:

> The womanhood of India will be with you as the holders of your banner, and the sustainers of your strength, and if you die remember that the spirit of Padmini of Chittoor (*sic*) is enshrined with the manhood of India.[43]

The 1917 session of the Indian National Congress was significant in the context of the Indian Women's Movement as it was presided over by Annie Besant, the first woman to do so. Besides Sarojini Naidu, another important woman participant was Begum Amman Bibi, mother of the brothers, Mohammad and Shaukat Ali. Describing the 1917 Congress, Margaret E. Cousins said, 'The three women were deeply significant in the new era in Indian social and political history. Womanhood had come out

Women students at a reception given to Gandhiji and Kasturba by Tagore in Shantiniketan, 1936

of its seclusion to share with manhood the struggle for gaining freedom for *Bharat Mata*, the Motherland.'[44] This new phase of the women's movement was further highlighted by the fact that a women's delegation led by Sarojini Naidu and organized by an Irish suffragette, Margaret Cousins (who was in India at the time), comprised 14 women who asked for better educational facilities, improved health and maternity benefits for women and asked for the same franchise rights 'as would be extended to their brothers'. These demands were placed before the Committee of the British government headed by Mr Montagu (the Secretary of State for India) and Lord Chelmsford, the Viceroy. Another delegation led by Sarla Devi Ghoshal, a Bengal reformer, also made representations before the committee on behalf of the *Bharat Stree Mahamandal*, one of the first women's political organizations in India (formed in 1910), which had branches in three important locations, Lahore, Allahabad and Calcutta.[45]

Another important event of 1917 was the formation of the *Women's Indian Association*. It was founded by Annie Besant,

Dorothy Jinarajadasa, Malati Patwardhan, Ammu Swaminathan, Mrs Dadabhoy and Mrs Ambujammal. The association was found at the height of the Home Rule Movement; even though the association was based in Madras, it had an all-India character. It was described as 'the first purely feminist organization to arise in India' by Rajkumari Amrit Kaur in 1932.[46] Needless to say such organizations had a 'multiplier' effect in the sphere of women's education. A logical outcome may be seen in a significant development that the All India Women's Conference (formed in 1927) expanded its scope and changed its name to the All India Women's Conference for Educational and Social Reform in 1929.

By the 1930s there were lively discussions on the quality of education to be imparted to girls. The generally accepted norm was to have a separate curriculum for girls with emphasis on the development of household skills and proficiency in drawing, painting and music. A different opinion was expressed by Rameshwari Nehru, prominent nationalist and journalist of Allahabad, who felt that education for women should be more broad-based. Education should not only enable a girl to become a good housewife and mother but also a good citizen and a good human being; it should, in addition, make her economically independent through training in crafts just like boys.[47] A more radical approach to women's education was expressed by Uma Nehru, another well-known activist of Allahabad, in an article 'Whither Women?':

> The decrepit, ignorant, helpless and insignificant woman of the past is giving place to the woman of the future, physically healthy, strong and enduring, morally a force and responsible member of society; intellectually man's equal if not superior; emotionally the centre of social life and economically the mistress of their own affairs.[48]

Gandhi's ideas on girl's education underwent considerable transformation over a period of time. Writing in *Hind Swaraj* in 1909 he says women ought to be 'queens of their households rather than "slaves" in factories'.[49] But in 1935 he insisted on the 'industrial education' of girls in order to make them self-reliant in all situations. In his scheme of 'Basic Education the all round development of boys and girls would be through vocational training in a handicraft and the syllabus would be woven around such training not in a mechanical but a scientific way. The child would then know the why and wherefore of every process. The products manufactured in the schools were to be bought by the state at prices fixed by it. In this way education would be self-financing. The boys and girls trained at these schools would be guaranteed employment by the state in the vocations they had learnt.' Gandhi was of the opinion that women could play an important role as teachers in this scheme. The women he had in mind were not needy women looking for jobs, but patriotic women with the leisure and zeal to serve the people and their country.[50]

Basic education in Gandhi's perception would lay the foundation of an egalitarian social order in which class conflict and the rural-urban divide would be replaced by all-round harmonious growth. For this purpose he advocated that the vocations through which the city children would receive their education ought to be directly related to the requirements of villages, just as village production had always been geared to the requirements of cities. This would, he said, check the progressive decay of the villages and make for a social order in which there was no unnatural division between the haves and the have-nots and everybody would be assured of a living wage and the right to freedom.[51] No doubt Gandhi's scheme was state-sponsored, but this did not deter him as he foresaw far-reaching social consequences if the scheme was implemented in the right spirit.

Between 1938 and 1939, several Basic Education Schools were set up, and in October 1939, the first conference of Basic National Education was held at Pune to review the progress of the scheme in its first year of working. Its report finally lifted the scheme above the realm of controversy and proved to the educational world that the claims of the new education system about the fundamental principles and contents and methods were justified by a year's experience of working with the teachers and the children. After independence, however, India's economic development took a different trajectory from the one visualized by Gandhi. As a result, the scheme languished and Basic Schools remained in name alone.[52] This does not in any way undermine the relevance of the scheme, which proved Gandhi's contention that education was not an end in itself but a means to an end.

NOTES

1. Sabyasachi Bhattacharya (ed.), *The Contested Terrain: Perspectives on Education in India*. Hyderabad: Orient Longman, 1998, p. 7.
2. Ibid, p. 131.
3. Krishna Kumar, *Political Agenda of Education: A Study of Colonialist and Nationalist Ideas*. New Delhi: Sage, 1991, pp. 124–136.
4. S. Bhattacharya, *The Contested Terrain*, pp. 39–40.
5. Ibid, p. 40.
6. Malabika Pande, *Gandhi's Vision of Social Transformation.* Jaipur: Rawat Publications, 2011, pp. 73–74.
7. Aparna Basu, 'National Education in Bengal: 1905–1912', in Bhattacharya, *The Contested Terrain*, p. 54.
8. Ibid, p. 57.
9 The Carlyle Circular was a secret communication issued on October 10, 1905 by R.W. Carlyle, Chief Secretary to the Government of Bengal to the Magistrates and Collectors instructing them to take stern measures to prevent students from joining the Boycott movement against the Partition of Bengal. S.N. Sen, *History of the Freedom Movement in India (1857-1947)*. New Delhi: New Age International, 1997, p. 100
10. Ibid, p. 59.
11. Ibid, p. 60.
12. Ibid, p. 62.

13. Radha Kumar, *The History of Doing: An Illustrated Account of Movements for Women's Rights and Feminism in India, 1800–1990*. New Delhi: Zubaan, 1993, p. 41.
14. Sumit Sarkar, *Swadeshi Movement in Bengal, 1903–08*. New Delhi: Peoples Publishing House, 1973, p. 192.
15. Manmohan Kaur, *Role of Women in the Freedom Struggle, 1857–1947*. Delhi: Sterling Publishers, 1968, p. 97.
16. Ibid, pp. 100–101.
17. Radha Kumar, *The History of Doing*, p. 42.
18. Madhu Kishwar, 'Arya Samaj and Women's Education – Kanya Mahavidyalaya, Jalandhar', in *Review of Women's* Studies, *Economic and Political Weekly*, Vol. XXI, No. 17, 26 April 1986 (pp. WS-9–WS-24), p. WS-18.
19. Ibid.
20. Manmohan Kaur, *Role of Women*, p. 98.
21. Aparna Basu, 'National Education in Bengal', p. 67.
22. *CWMG*, Vol. 18, p. 207.
23. Amrik Singh, 'Education and the National Movement', in Bhattacharya, *The Contested Terrain*, p. 71.
24. *CWMG*, Vol. 110, p. 302, 306.
25. A. Singh, 'Education and the National Movement', in Bhattacharya, *The Contested* Terrain, p. 75.
26. B.R. Nanda, *Gandhi: Pan Islamism, Nationalism and Imperialism*. Oxford: Oxford University Press, 1989, p. 189.
27. A. Singh, 'Education and the National Movement', in Bhattacharya, *The Contested Terrain*, p. 71, p. 76.
28. Ibid., p. 77.
29. Ibid., p. 99.
30. Ibid.
31. Ibid., pp. 80–81.
32. M. Pande, *Gandhi's Vision of Social Transformation*, pp. 72–73.
33. Bhattacharya, *The Contested Terrain*, p. 158.

34. M.K. Gandhi, *Educational Reconstruction*. Segaon Wardha: Hindustani Talimi Sangh, 1939, p. 34.
35. *Young India*, 27 April 1921.
36. M. Pande, *Gandhi's Vision of Social Transformation*, p. 168.
37. B.M. Sankhder, 'Gandhi and the National Educational Movement', in Bhattacharya, *The Contested Terrain*, p. 296.
38. Gandhi, 'Neither a Saint nor a Politician', *Young India 2* (12 May 1920), pp. 2–3.
39. R. Kumar, *The History of Doing*, p. 49; S. Sarkar, *Swadeshi Movement in Bengal*, p. 173.
40. Annie Besant, *Speeches & Writings*. Madras: G.A. Natesan, 1921, p. 73.
41. Sarojini Naidu, *Speeches and Writings*. Madras: G.A. Natesan, 1920, pp. 18–20.
42. Manmohan Kaur, *Role of Women*, p. 111.
43. Pattabhi Sitaramayya, *History of the Indian National Congress*, Vol. I. Delhi: S. Chand and Sons, 1936, p. 131.
44. R. Naidu, *Speeches and Writings*, p. 246.
45. S. Kumar, *The History of Doing*, pp. 53–54.
46. Ibid.
47. Quoted in Visalakshi Menon, *Indian Women and Nationalism: The UP Story*. New Delhi: Har-Anand Publications, 2003, p. 50.
48. Uma Nehru, 'Whither Women?', in Shyam Kumari Nehru (ed.), *Our Cause: A Symposium on Indian Women*. Allahabad: Kitabistan, 1952, pp. 413–415.
49. M.K. Gandhi, *Hind Swaraj or Indian Home Rule* (1909), edited by Anthony J. Parel. Cambridge: Cambridge University Press, 1997, p. 37.
50. M. Pande, *Gandhi's Vision of Social Transformation*, pp. 168–169.
51. Ibid.
52. Ibid, pp. 170–71.

CHAPTER 3

Women and the Nationalist Upsurge in Allahabad

Political mobilization of women in Allahabad was facilitated by the fact that from the beginning of the twentieth century Allahabad became the forerunner in the women's movement in United Provinces. The pioneer in this field was Mrs Rameshwari Nehru, wife of Shyam Lal Nehru, a senior government servant who was also a cousin of Jawaharlal Nehru. From 1909 Rameshwari began bringing out a women's magazine, *Stree Darpan* ('The Woman's Mirror'), which vividly reflected the social and legal problems afflicting Indian women and forcefully emphasized imperatives such as need for better education, inheritance rights, abolition of child marriage, divorce, remarriage of widows and right to vote. In one of the earlier issues of the magazine, issued in December 1911, an article on Hindu women stated that except on festivals like Dushera and Diwali, when they were ritually venerated by their husbands as Goddess Durga or Lakshmi, 'Hindu men worshipped their wives with brooms and despised them most of the time.'[1] *Stree Darpan* also discussed the contemporary political situation in a lucid manner, for example the significant role of women in the Bardoli Satyagraha of 1928.[2]

१ मार्च १९१०
भाग २
संख्या ३
स्त्री-दर्पण
सम्पादिका—
श्रीमती रामेश्वरी नेहरू
श्रीमती कमला नेहरू
वार्षिक
मूल्य २)
एक प्रति
मूल्य ।)

Rameshwari Nehru was the only woman appointed by the British government on a committee to fix the age of consent for girls,[3] an issue which had raised a national storm in 1891 when the Age of Consent Act was first passed. She was instrumental in organizing perhaps the first political meeting of women in 1916 in Allahabad. The subject was the inhuman treatment of Indian indentured labourers in South Africa. Gopal Krishna Gokhale, a liberal nationalist, had been mobilizing public support in the country for this cause. Vijaya Lakshmi Pandit, sister of Jawaharlal Nehru, recalls that 'it took consistent and patient effort for many days to persuade other women to speak.'[4] The efforts of the organizers were rewarded and the Mayo Hall of the University (*sic*), where the meeting was held, was packed to capacity.

After the Mayo Hall meeting, we find the *Prayag Mahila Samiti*, a women's group of Allahabad (founded by Rameshwari Nehru in 1909), organizing a public meeting on 18 February 1917 at Lala Bhawani Prasad's hall in Kooncha Sanwaldas to protest against the issue of indentured labour.[5] The establishment of the Home Rule League by Annie Besant with an office at Allahabad in 1916 provided an opportunity for women to engage in political questions. Vijaya Lakshmi Pandit, though only 16 years old at the time, eagerly read Mrs Besant's articles in her journals, *The Commonwealth* and *New India*, and enrolled as a volunteer in the Allahabad office of the Home Rule League.[6] Other women of the Nehru family, notably Swaroop Rani, Kamala and Uma (the wife of Jawaharlal's cousin Shamlal), also attended meetings of the League in Allahabad.[7]

Annie Besant's arrest in 1917 was the signal for mass mobilization in the United Provinces. Many public figures from zamindar, taluqdar and lawyer backgrounds joined the Home Rule League, and protest meetings were held in several districts. At the head of the campaign was C.Y. Chintamani, editor of *The Leader* (which was the most prominent nationalist English newspaper at the time in the United Provinces). *The Leader* reported that in Allahabad, Lucknow and Benaras special 'ladies meetings' expressing solidarity with Annie Besant were held on 4 July and 10 August 1917, which were well attended. At their gatherings, which were always held in the afternoon, women were exhorted to join the Home Rule League in large numbers. Annie Besant had indeed stirred public sympathy to a considerable extent in the United Provinces for the cause of Home Rule. Even so, women's political involvement in the United Provinces was relatively meagre till 1919; in fact, Rameshwari Nehru was lamenting in August 1919 that it was difficult to get women to come and attend meetings of the *Prayag Mahila Samiti*, which had to be held occasionally without the quorum![8]

Rameshwari Nehru (January 1953)

Gandhi's visit in November 1920, during his campaign of non-cooperation with the British Government, certainly hastened the political mobilization of women in Allahabad. At a women's meeting on 29 November, stating that swadeshi was not only relevant for the redress of the 'Punjab and *Khilafat* wrongs' but also the only effective way to swaraj, he affirmed that the main burden of propagating swadeshi lay on the women of India. In a spontaneous response to his speech many women gave away items of personal jewellery as donations to the national cause and simultaneously expressed enthusiasm about taking the vow of swadeshi.[9] On many occasions, using strong traditional imagery, Gandhi would tell the women that even Sita had worn rough clothes of tree bark during her exile of 14 years, including the period in Ravana's custody. In a similar manner, he expected women to wear khadi for liberating the country from British rule.[10] The impact of Gandhi's visit was visible from reports in *The Leader*. Thus, Shyam Kumari Nehru, eldest daughter of Uma Nehru, discontinued her studies at the Muir Central College.[11] Some 258 boys left and 13 teachers were reported to have resigned from government schools in Allahabad.[12]

Satyagraha as a method of national struggle had a special appeal for women for obvious reasons. Gandhi emphasized this point on his next visit to Allahabad in August 1921. At a public meeting at the Swaraj Sabha grounds attended by more than 10,000 people he declared that he expected more from women in terms of *swadeshi*, peaceful non-cooperation and communal amity because his religion was love, nonviolence and peace. He also urged women to shed their love of foreign cloth and asked everyone to make the *swadeshi* programme successful by September 1921 so that he could serve an ultimatum to the government. In a symbolic gesture Gandhi lit a huge bonfire of foreign cloth at the end of the meeting.[13]

The close interaction between Gandhi and the Nehru family in Allahabad was indeed instrumental in enabling the women of that family to take up positions of leadership in the initial stages of the struggle for freedom. Nehru women set an example by giving up all their fine imported clothes and wore heavy thick *khaddar*, the only kind available at the time, as a matter of principle.[14] When Jawahar Lal Nehru went to jail in 1921 for his part in the non-cooperation campaign, his mother Swaroop Rani declared, 'I rejoice in the great privilege of sending my dear husband and my only son to jail.'[15] Their absence, she added, would not stop the national struggle as the women would come forward to take their place. 'Were the jails of Mother India meant only for the men?' she had asked.[16]

Together with other women, Kamala Nehru, Uma Nehru and Swaroop Rani actively participated in the picketing of foreign cloth shops and protest meetings on 6 and 13 April 1921.[17] The District Magistrate of Allahabad had banned all public meetings for a week in view of the increasing political turmoil, but it was to defy this order that Swaroop Rani addressed a public meeting in the

Idgah. She held similar meetings on 8 April and in May 1921.[18] It was in recognition of her political role that Uma Nehru was elected member of the Executive Committee of the UP Congress Committee on 24 April 1921.[19] She was already in charge of the district *charkha* programme.[20] By May 1922, picketing of foreign cloth shops was so successful that Congress volunteers gave up picketing in Allahabad. Nearly all cloth merchants had signed the pledge not to stock foreign cloth.[21]

Figures for Allahabad are not available separately, but the success of the *swadeshi* movement can be gauged from the following all India figures: value of imports of foreign cloth fell from Rs. 102 crore in 1920–1921 to Rs. 57 crore in 1921–1922. Similarly, import of British piece goods fell from 1,291 million yards to 955 million yards.[22]

The Ahmedabad session of the Indian National Congress in December 1921 had an impact on far away Allahabad. It was at Gandhi's insistence that all the women of the Nehru family attended the session as most of the men were in jail. The experience of the train journey from Allahabad to Ahmedabad was like a 'triumphal procession' and the stay in Sabarmati Ashram left a deep impact even on a 14-year-old Krishna Nehru (the future Krishna Hutheesingh). She writes in her autobiographical work that life at the Ashram and seeing 'Bapu' from close quarters were 'sublime' experiences which would always remain fresh in her memory.[23]

An important development in the 1920s was the election of Uma Nehru on the Municipal Board of Allahabad and her subsequent election to the post of Chairperson of the Education Committee of the Board.[24] She was also a member of the Executive of the Provincial Congress Committee and in her spare time wrote on political issues for *Stree Darpan*.[25]

A combination of municipal initiative and private agency influenced by the Non-Cooperation Movement was responsible for a substantial expansion of educational opportunities for girls and women in Allahabad. Public-spirited figures like Bapu Sangam Lal Agarwal set up institutions such as the Prayag Mahila Vidyapith in the 1920s. The objective of this endeavour was to encourage girls who had passed the vernacular lower-middle examination to pursue higher studies in the same medium. At the beginning, the Mahila Vidyapith was only an examining body with a prescribed syllabus and conferred a series of degrees – *Praveshika*, which corresponded to the Middle School Leaving Certificate, *Vidya Vinodini* (High School / Matriculation), *Vidushi* (BA) and *Saraswati* (MA). These examinations were popular not only within UP but also in Bengal and Punjab.[26]

From 1932 onwards, the Prayag Mahila Vidyapith became a teaching institution, even providing hostel accommodation for women. The response was overwhelming, especially since a degree from the Vidyapith enabled them to find jobs as school teachers in private schools. Among the students at the Vidyapith were widows as well as the wives and daughters of Civil Disobedience Movement activists. The girls of the Mahila Vidyapith wore *Khadi* and the medium of instruction was Hindi.[27]

An important educational institution of Allahabad was the Crosthwaite Girls College which actually began as a school in Lucknow in 1895. The initiative was of Sayyid Karamat Husain, a lawyer who was committed to the cause of women's education. It received encouragement from Charles Crosthwaite, the then Lieutenant Governor of the Province and was named after him. However, it was soon shifted out of 'conservative' Lucknow to Allahabad where it flourished.[28] Prominent leaders of the time, such as Dr Tej Bahadur Sapru, Dr Sundar Lal and Pandit Braj Narayan Gurtu, were on its Managing Committee. In keeping with the times, strict *purdah* was observed in the school and all the teachers were 'ladies'. The school built a good reputation for itself and was closely associated with the nationalist developments in the city.[29] The *Stree Darpan*, the reputed journal of Allahabad mentioned earlier, reported the academic achievements of the school. In 1918, the school was preparing the students for the

Matriculation examination and had on its faculty one Ms K. Natarajan who had been recently appointed and had earlier taught history at the Madras Women's College.[30]

The appointment of the Simon Commission in 1927 galvanized political life in India after a hiatus of several years since 1922, even though this period had witnessed persistent communal turmoil. During the course of 1928, Youth Leagues under the leadership of Jawaharlal Nehru and Subhas Chandra Bose were formed across the country, which were radical and socialist in orientation. They pledged themselves to work for India's independence by mobilizing the villagers in rural areas.[31] In Allahabad, Krishna Nehru was the Joint Secretary of the Youth League, which soon became involved in the mass movement.[32]

Organizing women for political work on a large scale was begun by Kamala Nehru, wife of Jawaharlal, from 1928, when she started visiting individual homes in particular *mohallas* 'persuading, cajoling, inspiring the women to come out'. She fully appreciated the constraints of society on women and therefore began persuading the men to allow their women folk to come out of *purdah*.[33] She wrote to Dr Syed Mahmud, a family friend, 'I think all you men should be kept in *purdah* for a few years and then asked what you think of *purdah*.' By November 1929, Kamala's efforts bore such fruit that women of Allahabad presented the largest purse to Gandhi during his tour of the United Provinces. The cheque was for Rs. 8,000 and was given at a 'huge' meeting of women on 17 November 1929. This was followed by a big public meeting where the balance of the collections amounting to Rs. 10,000 was presented. The total for Allahabad District amounted to nearly Rs. 35,000, which Gandhi said was 'wholly unexpected'. He gave credit to Kamala Nehru, who though only recently discharged from hospital after a difficult operation, had taken up the onerous duty of Secretary of the Reception Committee and had in his words, 'given herself and her co-workers no rest'.[34]

The launch of the Salt Satyagraha on 6 April 1930 by Mahatma Gandhi was the signal for the widest participation of women in political activity on an all-India scale. In Allahabad, all through April 1930, salt was made at women's meetings in every *mohalla* in huge '*karahis*' (cooking pots) out of alkaline soil, on improvised wood fires and it was freshly packed in small pieces of paper (*purias*), and immediately auctioned for anything between Rs. 5 and Rs. 40. Kamaladevi Chattopadhyaya, a national-level Congress activist, confirms similar auctions in Bombay where women obtained salt from sea water carried in pitchers on their heads. At road crossings they would auction small quantities of the salt for large amounts of money.[35] The most popular spots in Allahabad for this unlawful activity were Kalyani Devi, Muthiganj, Moti Park, Ahiyapur and Katra, where women led huge processions which then transformed into meetings for salt-making, propagation of *khaddar*, collective oath-taking of the *swadeshi* pledge and enrolment of volunteers. At the end of the proceedings, often a bonfire of foreign cloth was lit as a symbolic gesture to mark the end of foreign rule. On such occasions women generally handed over their *chaadars* of foreign cloth to be burnt.[36]

Among the ladies who were spearheading the movement were Kamala Nehru, Uma Nehru, Swaroop Rani Nehru, Ramlalli Devi, Sundar Devi, Mrs Gurunarayan Khanna, Ganga Devi, Vijaya Lakshmi Pandit, Mrs P.D. Tandon, Vinodini Sinha, Tulsi Devi, Satyavati, Subhadra Devi and Mrs Rupnarayan Tripathi. In this earliest phase of the Civil Disobedience movement the government, as a matter of policy (quite apparently, the fear of aggravated consequences), did not arrest women *satyagrahis.*

As mentioned earlier the singing of national songs was an important element in the protocol of processions as it fuelled the enthusiasm of all participants. Apart from '*Jhanda Uncha Rahen Hamara*' and '*Sarfaroshi Ki Tamanna*', an emotive song of the time was:

> *Ai Madare Hind na ho gamgeen, din Achche aane wale hain.*
> *Azadi ka paigam tumhen ham jald sunane wale hain.*
> *Meri rooh ko karna kaidokafasha imkan se inke bahar hain.*
> *azad hai apana dil shaida go lakh juban par tale hain.*[37]

A free translation of the above lines would be:

> Do not be grieved Mother India, good days will come
> You shall soon hear the message of freedom from us
> They cannot capture my spirit, it is out of their control.
> My heart is free even though lakhs of tongues are locked.

Rural areas were also affected by the salt *satyagraha*. According to Lakshmi Kant Verma, well-known litterateur of Allahabad, women came out as if on pilgrimage to make salt in front of the *thanas* in open defiance of the law.[38]

From May (1930) onwards, the challenging task of picketing shops which sold foreign goods and liquor was undertaken, mainly by women. They came out in the 'blazing sun', directing volunteers, marching, attending meetings and standing for hours picketing shops. In this work Kamala Nehru was the 'uncrowned heroine'. Krishna Hutheesing writes: 'Kamala, whose fatal disease (TB) had returned, was the most active of all. She became the best organizer, the most intrepid marcher and the leading spirit of the women of Allahabad; up at 5 a.m. to drill volunteers and on the picket lines at eight.'[39]

Gyanwati Devi, Prabhavati Narayan and Vinodini Sinha were Kamala's co-workers. Vinodini and Gyanwati left their small children at home with neighbours or a maid. Picketing was a difficult job as the women were sometimes abused by both the shopkeepers and customers besides being dragged away by the police.[40] Sometimes a delicate situation would arise; this was dissuading Muslims who were accustomed to use cloth of a finer variety and of brighter colours than *khadi* could ever offer. Yet, Uma Nehru was successful in persuading many Muslim purchasers of cloth to buy only *swadeshi* cloth. Some of them left it to her decision to select the variety and choose the appropriate colour for them.[41]

The evening shift of picketing was often undertaken by Sushila Devi Yadav, Satyavati, Kala Devi, Vidyawati Tandon, Premlata, Shivkali, Raj Devi, Kishori Devi and Vijaya Lakshmi

Pandit. Some women in both groups did double shifts.[42] It was not as if the women volunteers faced no opposition from their families. Often patriarchal attitudes did indeed come in the way of their participation. Kamala Nehru and her team had to continuously visit the homes of women and persuade their men folk that there was nothing unseemly about women picketing cloth shops.[43]

An important achievement, as far as the goal of *swadeshi* was concerned, was getting bales of foreign cloth sealed, which Kamala Nehru was able to accomplish after a lot of persuasion and applying pressure of picketing on the merchants concerned. She also formed an association of women with the objective of teaching them to spin and to hold meetings and discussions once a week. Teachers were employed for this purpose. To propagate the message of *swadeshi* she and her co-workers like Vinodini, Prabhavati and Gyanwati, decided to take out an all-women procession with the participants holding *taklis* in their hands. Though it was drizzling on that day, women in large numbers came out to join the procession.[44]

Large-scale picketing by the women soon began to produce results especially in areas like Daraganj, Khuldabad and Chowk. In fact foreign cloth largely disappeared from shops in Chowk.[45] Newspapers reported that Japan, Britain, France and Germany were all worried over their exports because of the boycott movement in India.[46] Sumit Sarkar states that there was indeed 'a remarkable fall in British cloth imports from 26 million pounds in 1929 to 13.7 million pounds in 1930 and quantity wise from 1248 million yards in 1929-30 to only 523 million yards in 1930-31.' Other British imports also suffered.[47]

Some acts of individual heroism need to be recorded. Vinodini Sinha while collecting donations for the *satyagraha* movement, marched into the Kotwali in Chowk and harangued and shamed the Indian Kotwal (an officer of the British Government) into giving a donation, though from the hands of his wife. He then begged her to leave for fear of losing his job. Vinodini cites this incident as the reason for her not being arrested even once during the movement. On another occasion she was persuading a merchant to surrender his stock of foreign cloth when he taunted her for wearing foreign-made bangles. She immediately picked up the steel measuring rod and broke her bangles in full public view even though such an act is traditionally done only when a Hindu woman becomes a widow.[48]

An unique feature of the Civil Disobedience Movement in Allahabad was the *Vanar Sena* or Monkey Brigade whose chief organizer was 13-year-old Indira Nehru. The headquarters of the Sena was at the Anand Bhavan, her own ancestral house. Krishna Hutheesing relates an interesting fact about its functioning. As there were several thousand children volunteers in the Sena, Indira devised a novel method of being heard while speaking, that is, by using 'human loudspeakers'. She would shout a sentence and a boy or a girl in the crowd would turn and bellow it to those further back and so on. The 'monkeys' proved very useful as they took over jobs like addressing envelopes, making flags, carrying messages, gathering intelligence unnoticed and unsuspected by the police.[49]

Activists in the *Vanar Sena*, like Mrs Manorama Shukla[50] and Mrs Savitri Wattal,[51] recall that they would march, singing national songs, sell small packets of freshly manufactured contraband salt and hand over big donations to the National Fund. They would also vie with each other to give away foreign toys and garments to be burnt in the bonfires; shout slogans like *Vandemataram* and *Todi Baccha Hai Hai* ('Down with Toadies') on seeing white soldiers which would irritate them intensely. Mrs Shukla recalls that teachers of her school, Arya Kanya Pathshala, would accompany their processions and during the Kumbh Mela of 1931 the 'monkeys' tried to persuade the pilgrims to give up foreign cloth, entered shops with the same purpose and some shopkeepers even gave away their stocks of foreign cloth willingly.

An important organization called the *Desh Sevika Sangh* was formed by some women of Allahabad under the presidentship of Uma Nehru. This body had several wings which looked after different activities. Picketing was the responsibility of Uma Nehru; liquor boycott of Vijaya Lakshmi Pandit, women volunteers of Krishna Nehru and *Prabhat Pheris* of Shyam Kumari Nehru. In November 1931 a branch of the Provincial *Desh Sevika Sangh* was opened in Allahabad with its office near Bharti Bhavan in Chowk. Kamala Nehru became the president of this branch while Maina Devi and another lady were its office bearers.[52]

At the Women's Political Conference of the United Provinces it was Kamala Nehru who presided and from that platform she made a special appeal to the women of Allahabad to make the national movement successful. Soon she was appointed President of the Allahabad Congress Committee and in addition the local Congress 'dictator', that is, the activist in charge of Civil Disobedience activities.[53]

Meanwhile Civil Disobedience gathered greater momentum, more volunteers enrolled every day, women's meetings grew in size; not a single student attended class in the Allahabad University for some time, while the government grew worried over the 'increasing mischief' and economic losses.[54]

Women soon became involved with the students' movement in Allahabad. After the arrest of Gandhi on 5 May 1930 angry students in Allahabad began picketing schools and colleges to force their closure as a mark of sympathy. The Principal of Modern School misbehaved with the boys who were trying to picket his school and soon the situation turned violent. Kamala Nehru was called immediately and she managed to diffuse the situation. As a sequel to this incident a students' union was formed and Kamala Nehru became its Treasurer, and Vijaya Lakshmi its Secretary. In the Executive Committee of the Union there were two representatives from each school.[55]

The increasing political mobilization of women forced the British Government to change its earlier policy of not arresting women. The first to be arrested were Krishna Nehru and Shyam Kumari Nehru on 11 November 1930 for attending unlawful meetings and processions. They were sentenced to one month's imprisonment or they could pay a fine of Rs. 100, but as Congress policy was to refuse to pay fines they both accepted imprisonment. An unknown person paid the fine on behalf of Krishna Nehru and much to her consternation she was released.[56] Soon it was Kamala's turn to be arrested. In December 1930 she began touring villages in order to mobilize peasants to withhold rent and revenue and to boycott foreign goods. She addressed a meeting at Bardhaga village, Bazar Karma in Karchana Tehsil on 26 December 1930, which was attended by 4,000 to 5,000 people. As such meetings had been declared illegal, and she was arrested and sentenced to six months simple imprisonment.[57]

Apart from the Nehru women, others began to be arrested from November 1930 for picketing. Seven women were arrested; one of them had a daughter who was to be married in a few days time. She, along with the others, was given three months rigorous imprisonment.[58] All this had a positive impact, and there was soon a surplus of female volunteers for picketing, so much so that Uma Nehru who was the organizer even announced that there was no need for any male volunteers.[59]

There was a temporary suspension of the Civil Disobedience Movement as a result of the Gandhi–Irwin Pact in February 1931. Most of the political prisoners, including Kamala Nehru, were released at this time. But the negotiations during the Second Round Table Conference in England failed and with Gandhi's return to India in early January 1932, Civil Disobedience was resumed with greater vigour. The new Conservative government in Britain was determined to crush the movement with all its might and armed the Indian government with the necessary powers by means of special laws and ordinances.

Soon most of the Congress leaders were in jail and their place outside was taken by the women. From early January 1932 it became almost a daily routine for women activists including

Women activists led by Swaroop Rani Nehru and Kamala Nehru making Salt, Allahabad 1930

Swaroop Rani, Uma Nehru, Vijaya Lakshmi Pandit, Purnima Banerji, Krishna Nehru and dozens of others to march in procession from Khaddar Bhandar (in Chowk) towards Civil Lines. But every time they were stopped by the police near the P.D. Tandon Park from advancing further. On these occasions they would all sit down on the road, sing national songs or some would address the crowd but none would move from her place. Vijaya Lakshmi recalls, 'this situation sometimes went on for hours'. Finally arrests of the leader with a couple of hundred others followed and the procession dispersed for the day.[60]

Uma Nehru was arrested on 9 January 1932. In mid-January Swaroop Rani, Purnima Banerji, Vijaya Lakshmi Pandit and Krishna Nehru were served with an injunction against taking part in any public meeting.[61] They decided to obey the order for the time being as a great meeting had been planned for 'Independence Day', 26 January 1932, less than two weeks away. Mrs Pandit was the 'dictator' of the Allahabad City Congress; she presided over the meeting held at P.D. Tandon Park and the *Independence Pledge* was taken by the assembled crowd, many of whom sat on 'branches of trees' for lack of space. Swaroop Rani though frail and old gave a 'fiery speech' which 'swayed and roused the vast crowd to a peak of high emotion'. Police disrupted the meeting with a sudden *lathi* charge; many were injured and arrested there and then. Among the women arrested were Purnima Banerji,[62] Prabhavati Narayan, Gyanwati Devi, Mania Devi and Ramkali Jaiswal. Vijaya Lakshmi Pandit and Krishna Nehru were arrested the next morning from Anand Bhawan. All the women were sentenced to one year's rigorous imprisonment, but Mrs Pandit was awarded an additional fine of Rs. 300. She refused to pay as was expected; hence, her term in prison was extended by six weeks.[63] It is worth noting that Gyanwati Devi went to prison with her three-month-old child, which became quite a norm for activists with small children!

The spate of arrests of women political activists continued. In April 1932, *National Week* (6 to 13 April) was observed to commemorate Jalianwala Bagh and other 'massacres'. On the night of 9 April many women participated in the procession which proceeded from the city side to Civil Lines. At the junction of Canning Road and Stanley Road the police ordered them to stop whereupon 'the *Satyagrahis* sat down in the middle of the road, sang Congress songs and shouted revolutionary slogans'. As a huge crowd of spectators collected, the police suddenly ordered a *lathi* charge followed by firing. Many of the demonstrators were injured while some were killed. Mrs Swaroop Rani Nehru received serious head injuries.[64] Among the women who were arrested and convicted were Mrs Ram Rati, Lakshmi Devi, Saraswati Devi and Rajendra Kishori. They were sentenced to six months rigorous imprisonment and ordered to pay fines of Rs. 200 each, in default of which their term in prison was to be extended by six weeks. Rajendra Kishori went to prison with two small children.[65] Two other women Kusuma Devi Bhatt and Sundar Devi had also been arrested, but they were released soon as they tendered apologies for participating in the procession.[66] Social compulsions often forced women to take this step.

Some women activists used an alias to escape the rigours of distraint. One such was Mrs Ketaki Bhatt (daughter-in-law of well-known litterateur Bal Krishna Bhatt) who used the alias 'Saraswati Devi'. Pratibha Malaviya, daughter of Ketaki Bhatt, recalled that her mother was at all times prepared for arrest. Tri-colour flags and symbols of freedom were stitched by the women activists in the upper hall of a shop in Chowk, referred to as Jha's shop, and almost every participant carried a flag. The rule was never to surrender the flag but hand it over to another *satyagrahi* before being arrested. Ketaki Bhatt, after her arrest on 9 April 1932 fell ill in Lucknow Central Jail, where she had been transferred and was told by the prison authorities to ask for pardon so that she could be released. She refused this offer and served her full term in prison.[67]

In order to restrict the increasing participation of women in the national movement in 1932, the government decided to discourage them by awarding long sentences and subjecting them to harsh treatment in jail.[68] For instance, a number of girls, mostly 15 or 16 years old, who met in a private house in Allahabad to discuss what they could do for the movement, were arrested from the house and each of them was sentenced to two years rigorous imprisonment.[69] This was a common occurrence all over India. Nehru writes: 'Most of the girls and women who were sentenced had a very bad time in prison, even worse than the men had.'

But such repression did not deter women from carrying on their political activities. On 31 May 1932, Mrs Vidya Malaviya managed to escape the police dragnet and was able to hold a meeting at Ghantaghar Chowk. She was subsequently arrested and awarded rigorous imprisonment for one year.[70]

Mrs Kamla Devi Sharma was the 'dictator' of the Allahabad Town Congress Committee when it was decided to hold a 'boycott

Kamla Devi Sharma

day' on 28 August 1932. Leaflets were distributed for the purpose, and in the morning and in the evening she led processions of volunteers, carrying national flags and singing revolutionary songs in the city centre in Ghantaghar. When she was arrested at the crossing of Hewitt Road and City Road she immediately handed over the flag and leadership to a volunteer with instructions to take the procession to Mohammad Ali Park. Kamla Devi was ordered to pay a fine of Rs. 200, which she refused; in default she suffered simple imprisonment for six weeks.[71]

Life in jail was not altogether bleak for the Congress women. Some women were able to complete their education while in jail. For example Purnima Banerji (sister of Aruna Asaf Ali) completed her BA degree while in prison; others who had begun their studies in jail went on to complete it after their jail term came to end.[72]

Vijaya Lakshmi Pandit was arrested, along with her sister Krishna, on 26 January 1932. For three days they were in Allahabad District Jail, which she describes as 'a collection of mud houses in a large yard enclosed by a dilapidated wall'. 'Prostitutes' were the main occupants of the female section apart from some others who had been arrested for petty thefts. Though initially shocked, she and others like her learnt to accept such women. After their trial, the Nehru sisters were transferred to Lucknow Central Jail and accorded 'A Class' status by a magistrate who, she says, was extremely nervous as he had never before had to deal with women 'politicals'.[73]

Krishna's account of the Allahabad District jail was more graphic: 'The first few days were a novel experience and one that none of us can ever forget. Our cells had all sorts of insects crawling around and for several nights we could not sleep for fear that these beastly things might get into our beds... Later on we had a general clean-up, before retiring each night and nothing untoward happened for the rest of our stay there.'[74]

The Civil Disobedience Movement abated during 1933 and was finally suspended in 1934. Attention now shifted to 'constructive' activities. Serious efforts to improve civic amenities were made by two women who managed to find a place for themselves on the Municipal Board of Allahabad in the mid-1930s. Vijaya Lakshmi Pandit was elected from the Congress Party, which secured a majority on the Board. Mrs Pratibha Banerji, a prominent social worker, was the government nominee. Mrs Pandit was also elected chairperson of the Education Committee of the Municipal Board. Apart from initiating a fresh approach by insisting on personal visits to the municipal schools and meetings with the teachers she is remembered for inaugurating a novel 'milk scheme' for the children of the municipal schools.[75] She also made an attempt to improve the condition of the night schools for adults run by the Board by turning them into community centres.

Another dimension of women's political mobilization began with the founding of the Congress Socialist Party (CSP) in Bombay in 1934. The party was the result of interaction between Communists and Congress activists in jail who realized that for the moment the mass movement was over. In the UP organization of the party there were five women, namely, Viddottama Devi from Bareilly, Purnima Banerji and Hajra Begum from Allahabad, Ms Tailang in Benaras and Lakshmi Devi in Ghazipur.[76] The Allahabad women were known to work among the press workers and railway coolies.[77]

In the elections of 1937, under the new system of provincial autonomy, the Indian National Congress came to power in seven of the 11 British provinces and remained in office till they resigned in 1939 on the issue of India's forced participation in the Second World War. Of the 13 women elected to the new Legislative Assembly of the United Provinces convened at Lucknow, two – Uma Nehru and

Vijaya Lakshmi Pandit – were from Allahabad. Mrs Pandit was also the first woman to be appointed as a Cabinet Minister in any province in India; she held the portfolio of Local Self-Government and Public Health. Besides launching a drive to curb extravagance and corruption in the departments, her personal achievement was to start, in the face of stiff opposition from officialdom and even some colleagues, the first clinic for pregnant women suffering from venereal diseases.[78] Hajra Begum and Purnima Banerji of the CSP were also active at this time, organizing *kisan* (farmers) processions and rural meetings around Allahabad.[79]

By January 1940, up to 10,000 women were enrolled as members of the Congress in the United Provinces. Uma Nehru was in charge of the women's wing, and their involvement was mainly in the 'constructive' programme of the Congress. This comprised of *swadeshi*, eradication of untouchability, removal of illiteracy and enrolment of new members in the Congress.[80]

Tried and tested women came forward to register their protest during the individual *satyagraha* campaign launched by Mahatma Gandhi in 1940. The objective of the individual *satyagraha* was to establish the right of freedom of speech and to register India's protest against her forced participation in the Second World War. The prospective *satyagrahi* would have to publicly declare: 'It is wrong to help the British war effort with men or money. The only worthy effort is to resist all war with non-violent resistance.' The *satyagrahi* would beforehand inform the District Magistrate of the time and place where he or she was going to make the antiwar speech. If the government did not arrest the *satyagrahi* he or she would not only repeat the performance but move into the villages and start a trek towards Delhi.[81]

Raj Rani Nishad, who belonged to a backward community in the Daraganj locality, went to prison for three-and-a-half months for her participation in individual *satyagraha*. Influenced by Mrs Purnima Banerji, Raj Rani became fully involved in the national movement. She received two awards for maximum enrolment of Congress members in Daraganj. To propagate the cause of *swadeshi* she not only plied the *charkha* but also distributed *taklis* and cotton among the local women, received yarn in return and gave them equal value of *khaddar*. In the course of this activity she involved Muslim women who generally suffered from *purdah* restrictions.[82]

Mania Devi, Gyanwati Devi and Vinodini Sinha who had been actively involved in the Civil Disobedience Movement of 1930 and 1932 were also active in the *individual satyagraha* campaign but did not go to jail. Purnima Banerji was arrested on 17 November 1940 for distributing copies of the proscribed statement of Jawaharlal Nehru given some time ago at the time of his arrest. Vijaya Lakshmi Pandit was arrested in December 1940 in Kanpur as soon as she gave notice to the authorities of the time and place of the proposed *satyagraha*. Both the ladies were sent to Naini Central Prison to serve their sentences.[83] Sushila Devi and Meenakshi Devi were arrested from the village of Dharia as soon as they gave notice to the authorities for undertaking individual *satyagraha*.[84]

It was the *Quit India* Movement of 1942 that again brought about a high level of political mobilization of women despite its revolutionary nature. The sudden arrest of all the national leaders, including Gandhi, in the early hours of 9 August 1942 in Bombay and their being taken away to an unknown destination provoked the Indian people beyond measure. There was a spontaneous outburst of public protests led by students all over the country, which quickly turned into an underground and violent movement due to excessive repression by the British government.

Rameshwari Nehru's appeal to the women of the Provinces, under the title *Striyon se Appeal*, illustrates her keen understanding of the critical situation before the country. In her appeal she explained that after the arrest of Mahatma Gandhi and other Congress leaders it was now the responsibility of ordinary men and women to carry on the struggle. She suggested the following activities for women:

1. Carrying messages from one part of the city to the other.
2. Taking Congress bulletins and circulars to required places.

3. Conducting house-to-house propaganda for the cause.
4. Refusing to work as domestic help in the houses of government officials.
5. Establishing contacts with policemen in order to persuade them not to take action against agitators.
6. Organizing first-aid for those injured in lathi charges and other repressive actions.[85]

Most of the activities suggested, though considered common-place by the nationalists, were in the prohibited category at the time.

In Allahabad, Vijaya Lakshmi Pandit was among the first to be arrested in the early hours of 13 August 1942, the day after the police fired on a procession of university students, leading to the death of one boy, Lal Padamdhar. Mrs Pandit had been in close touch with the students' movement and underground activists like Lal Bahadur Shastri and members of the Congress Socialist Party (CSP). Just before her arrest she was planning to secretly distribute leaflets prepared by the socialists carrying instructions for the rural areas.[86] The arrest of Mrs Pandit was followed by that of many women and young girls. All political prisoners were now to be classed as Q (for *Quit India*) and be given second-class treatment. None of the earlier privileges like books, visits, were to be permitted; they would have to wear clothes provided by the jail authorities and the daily food allowance was reduced from twelve annas a day to nine.[87]

On 24 August 1942, three women volunteers were brought to the Naini prison. One was a person Mrs Pandit refers to as wife of R.M.S. who came with her seven-year-old daughter. The second was Purnima Banerji and the third Urmila Tripathi, against whom there were charges of loot and arson. The charges, according to Mrs Pandit, must have been false as Urmila was not only a timid person but appeared disinterested in politics. Janki Devi, a widow and a teacher, came to prison on the 25th, charged with looting and arson at a rural station in Allahabad district. Janki Devi, according to Mrs Pandit, was a committed and enlightened nationalist who could not have indulged in such rowdyism. Repression appears to have been let loose by the government. Chandralekha, 18-year-old daughter of Mrs Pandit, who also had been active in the student's movement, joined her mother in prison on 30 August 1942.[88]

Defying the Ordinances imposed by the government, Indira Gandhi called a meeting at the Ghantaghar in Chowk and just as it was about to begin the police came to arrest her. Indira refused to submit tamely; as a result there was a scuffle between her supporters, herself and the police, in which she, among others, was injured and her clothes got torn. It was in this condition that she was brought to prison with her supporters on September 11, 1942.[89] The other women who accompanied her to prison included Ram Kali Jaiswal, Mahadevi Chaubey, Laxmi Bapat, a young girl called Vidyapati who was pregnant, and Govindi Devi only 12 years old. Ram Kali Jaiswal was a remarkable woman; not only was her husband in jail, but her young, ailing son was also in jail for his political activities.[90] Some of the women activists, including Mrs Pandit, Indira Gandhi and Chandralekha (daughter of Mrs Pandit), fell ill in jail, but none were prepared to apologize just to be released.

More and more young women continued to join the national movement and were sent to jail. On 1 October 1942, Kalavati Misra came to prison with her two-year-old child. Her husband, a Congress worker, was already in jail; their two young children were at home with her mother-in-law. She was arrested while on her way to join a procession with the tricolour flag in her hand. Kalavati, an old lady now, recalls that she was first inspired by Purnima Banerji whom she met at her school for adult women. Soon she began to accompany her on her political missions. In prison, Kalavati's child was looked after by Purnima and Indira Gandhi who arranged for food and milk from Anand Bhawan.[91]

Ram Kali's commitment to the cause of India's freedom was so complete that the deepest personal tragedy did not upset her. Her 16-year-old son who was ailing in prison was suddenly released as his condition worsened but she did not ask to be released herself to look after him. Ram Kali was in any case released before the expiry of her term and was with her son when he expired in June 1943. Soon she was back in prison for civil disobedience.[92]

The Congress' role in mobilizing various sections of the population was in evidence when a Harijan woman by the name of Dubasi came to prison for the second time on 22 October 1942. Her husband was also a Congressman in Barokhar.[93] Female students of Allahabad University were highly visible in the Quit India campaign. Chandralekha, daughter of Mrs Pandit, was already in prison. Chinta Malaviya, granddaughter of Madan Mohan Malaviya, and Vimla Verma came to prison on 1 November 1942. Kanti Sharma, another BA student, was sent to prison on 26 November 1942.[94]

Jail life for women prisoners of the Quit India Movement was much harder than in earlier movements. They received second-class (Q) treatment, which was an attempt to discourage them from participation, an attempt which did not succeed. Vijaya Lakshmi Pandit in her writings about her prison life said that initially her morale was low, 'but over the wall from the men's prison came shouts of *Inquilab Zindabad* ('Long Live Revolution'). It was like a shot in the arm, and the slogan revived me more than food could have done. It seemed that a great many political prisoners were being brought in at short intervals, for again and again the exuberant shouts came to me. This was good news.'[95] Another experience was that of Purnima Banerji who wrote to Jawaharlal Nehru about it: 'Prisons are really futile institutions, they change nobody. They neither succeed in chastising nor repressing.'[96]

Krishna Nehru, in her prison days, found herself empathizing with the many young women who had been convicted for crimes that they barely understood. She wrote, 'I was very glad to have been able to make friends with some of those convicts who were considered a menace to society, but who were far better specimens of humanity than many of the people we come across in our daily life.' She was deeply worried about their future.[97] There were also mixed experiences for other Congress women in jail. Women from orthodox families like that of Madan Mohan Malaviya tried to follow their orthodox practices even in jail. Reacting to this, Vijaya Lakshmi Pandit writes impatiently: 'I do not know what urge led them to participate in a movement, the whole purpose of which was to break down barriers and create a new social and political order.'[98]

An important activity undertaken by the students was looking after the families of political prisoners and underground activists, by forming Relief Committees. Mrs Kamla Bahuguna recalls that students like herself collected donations for this purpose and personally visited their homes to reassure them of their support. Mrs Purnima Banerji was their guide in these matters and some of the other girls were the Malaviya sisters – Daya, Chinta and Kumud – and the Verma sisters – Nirmala, Prabha and Vimla. According to Mrs Bahuguna, two women, Ms Das and Ms Kochar, were actively involved in the underground movement which published and distributed proscribed literature and also undertook terrorist missions against the British government. Her own house, Kamla Bahuguna said, used to be a centre of underground activity and was raided by the police on 24 October 1942, but nothing incriminating was found as all evidence had been removed in time.[99]

Another significant activity undertaken by many women during the movement of 1942 was the provision of food and shelter to the underground activists. Although this task involved high risks it was undertaken as a matter of pride by these women. Ketaki Bhatt who had been very active in the earlier Civil Disobedience Movement was physically unable to participate in the movement of 1942, but at her house in Ahiyapur underground activists were always assured of food and shelter. Her daughter Pratibha and son-in-law, Manohar Malaviya (also known as Azad), actively helped in this work.[100]

The years between 1916 and 1942 reveal a marked growth in the political mobilization of women in Allahabad. In conclusion it may not be out of place to quote Vijaya Lakshmi Pandit's personal assessment of the women's situation: 'The emergence of Indian women as an important flank of the national movement had been yet another example of the magic of Gandhiji. His call to women had been answered by thousands, crossing all traditional barriers of creed and caste and encompassing all social and economic levels – Indian women had achieved a sense of equality denied by immemorial custom.'[101]

NOTES

1. *Stree Darpan*, Vol. I, File I, Hindi Sahitya Sammelan Sangrahalaya (Allahabad), pp. 333–343.
2. An issue of 1928.
3. Vijaya Lakshmi Pandit, *The Scope of Happiness: A Personal Memoir*. Delhi: Vikas Publishing House, 1979, p. 31. The Act amended the Indian Penal Code and the Code of Criminal Procedure to raise the age of sexual relations for married and unmarried girls from 10 years (the age specified in this regard in the Indian Penal Code of 1860) to 12 years.
4. Ibid., p. 61.
5. *The Leader*, 17 February 1918, p. 5.
6. V.L. Pandit, *The Scope of Happiness*, p. 62.
7. Dr Sandhya Nagar, Archival Officer, State Archives, Lucknow, 'Contribution of Women of Allahabad in the Freedom Struggle' (unpublished, n.d.). Swaroop Rani and Kamala, the mother and the wife of Jawaharlal Nehru, were celebrated nationalist activists in their own right.
8. Visalakshi Menon, *Indian Women and Nationalism: The UP Story*. New Delhi: Har-Anand Publications, 2003, p. 63.

9. *The Leader*, December 1, 1920.
10. Uma Rao, 'Women in the Frontline: The case of U.P.', in Leela Kasturi and Vina Mazumdar (eds), *Women and Indian Nationalism*. New Delhi: Vikas Publishing House, 1994, pp. 28–52, p. 33.
11. *The Leader*, 21 November 1928, p. 5.
12. *The Leader*, 30 March 1921, p. 9.
13. *CWMG*, Vol. 20, pp. 485–486.
14. V.L. Pandit, *The Scope of Happiness*, p. 82.
15. B.R. Nanda, *The Nehrus*. London: George Allen and Unwin, p. 196.
16. Nagar, 'Contribution of Women of Allahabad'.
17. V.L. Pandit, *The Scope of Happiness*, p. 83.
18. Nagar, 'Contribution of Women of Allahabad'.
19. *The Leader*, 4 May 1921, p. 6.
20. *Stree Darpan*, November, 1921.
21. *The Leader*, 7 May 1922, p. 7.
22. Sumit Sarkar, *Modern India 1885–1947*. Delhi: Macmillan, 1983, p. 207.
23. Krishna Hutheesing, *We Nehrus*. Bombay: Pearl Books, 1967, pp. 58–59.
24. V.L. Pandit, *The Scope of Happiness*, p. 32.
25. *Stree Darpan*, September 1920, November 1921.
26. V. Menon, *Indian Women and Nationalism*, p. 39.
27. Ibid.
28. Ibid., p. 42.
29. Ibid., p. 43.
30. *Stree Darpan*, 1 June 1918.
31. Gyanendra Pandey, *The Ascendancy of the Congress in Uttar Pradesh: A Study in Imperfect Mobilisation, 1926–1934*. Delhi: Oxford University Press, 1978, pp. 164–65.
32. Menon, *Indian Women and Nationalism*, p. 79.

33. From Dr Uma Rao's unpublished monograph on Kamala Nehru, sponsored by the Kamala Nehru Trust, p. 50.
34. CWMG, Vol. 42, p. 218.
35. Radha Kumar, *The History of Doing: An Illustrated Account of Movements for Women's Rights and Feminism in India, 1800–1990.* New Delhi: Zubaan, 1993, p. 78.
36. Files of *Satyagraha Samachar*, which were 1 paisa news sheets on the progress of civil disobedience in the country, brought out by the Satyagraha Committee of Prayag, edited by Baijnath Kapoor, printed at Abhyudaya Press, Allahabad, from April 1930. The files are available at the U.P. State Archives, Lucknow.
37. This song was recollected during interview with Late Mrs Pratibha Malaviya, daughter of well-known freedom fighter Ketaki Bhatt, and an activist herself.
38. *The Leader*, 4 May 1930, p. 10.
39. Hutheesing, *We Nehrus*, p. 91.
40. Uma Rao, 'Women in the Frontline', p. 56.
41. *The Leader*, 4 May 1930, p. 10.
42. Uma Rao, 'Women in the Frontline', p. 55.
43. Interview with Prabhavati Narayan, OHT, NMML, p. 17.
44. Uma Rao, 'Women in the Frontline', p. 54.
45. *Satyagraha Samachar* files, 4 and 9 May 1930.
46. Ibid., May 10, 1930.
47. S. Sarkar, *Modern India 1885–1947*, p. 293.
48. Interview with Vinodini Sinha by Dr Uma Rao.
49. K. Hutheesing, *We Nehrus*, p. 92.
50. Interview with Late Mrs Manorama Shukla on 31 December 96 at her residence in Bank Road, Allahabad.
51. Interview on 10 July 1998 at her residence in Tagore Town, Allahabad. She has also written an article on *Vanar Sena* in *Chinarika*, an annual magazine of the Kashmiri Samaj issued on the occasion of *Navreh*, 29 March 1998 from Allahabad.

52. Promilla Kalhan, *Kamala Nehru: An Intimate Biography*. Delhi: Vikas Publishing House, 1973, pp. 58–61.
53. S. Nagar 'Contribution of Women of Allahabad'.
54. *Satyagraha Samachar*, files of 28 April to 4, 7, 9, 10, 31 May, June 9 and 4 and 8 August 1930, Regional Archives, Lucknow.
55. *Satyagraha Samachar*, 6 May 1930.
56. K. Hutheesing, *We Nehrus*, p. 93.
57. Allahabad Regional Archives, S.L. No. 5, File No. 52.
58. *Abhyudaya*, 25 November 1930, p. 1 and 30 November 1930, p. 1.
59. V.L. Pandit, *The Scope of Happiness*, p. 101.
60. Ibid., p. 108; Allahabad Regional Archives, S.L. No. 24, File No. 74.
61. K. Hutheesing, *We Nehrus*, p. 64.
62. Allahabad Regional Archives, S.L. No. 8, File No. 72.
63. Jawaharlal Nehru, *An Autobiography*. New Delhi: Oxford University Press, 1980, p. 335.
64. Allahabad Regional Archives, S.L. No. 95, File No. 39.
65. Allahabad Regional Archives, S.L. No. 85, File No. 43.
66. Interview with Late Mrs Pratibha Malaviya, at her residence in Ahiyapur on 11 June 1996. According to Pratibha Malaviya, Ketaki Bhatt spent her leisure time in jail learning Urdu; she already knew Bengali and Gujarati in addition to her mother tongue, Hindi.
67. J.L. Nehru, *An Autobiography*, p. 330.
68. Ibid.
69. S. Nagar 'Contribution of Women of Allahabad'.
70. Allahabad Regional Archives, S.L. No. 103, File No. 542.
71. Menon, *Indian Women and Nationalism*, p. 154.
72. Pandit, *The Scope of Happiness*, p. 103.
73. Ibid.
74 Krishna Hutheesing, *With No Regrets: An Autobiography*. Bombay: Padma Publications, 1944, p. 66.

75. V.L. Pandit, *The Scope of Happiness*, p. 124. When donations for the milk scheme did not come from the wealthy bankers and businessmen of the city, she issued an appeal ward-wise for one penny from each home every month to build up a 'milk fund'. Friends and colleagues gave generous donations, but it was 'the pennies which poured in and filled to overflowing the little wooden boxes we had put up in each mohalla and the milk scheme was inaugurated', she wrote. Even after she left office, the milk scheme continued for some years afterward, mostly on penny donations.
76. J.P. Narayan Papers, CSP File 35, List of U.P. CSP Members, District-wise.
77. Hajra Begum, *Oral History Transcripts*, Nehru Memorial Museum and Library, p. 46.
78. V.L. Pandit, *The Scope of Happiness*, p. 137.
79. *Police Abstracts of Intelligence*, U.P. No. 33/1937, p. 21, August, p. 551.
80. Files of *Chaand* magazine, issue of February 1940, available at Hindi Sahitya Sammelan, Allahabad.
81. Bipan Chandra et al., *India's Struggle for Independence*. New Delhi: Penguin Books, 1989, p. 453.
82. Interview with Late Raj Rani Nishad at her residence in Daraganj, March 1996. She remained politically active and was elected Congress Corporator of the Municipality along with Purnima Banerjee. She has also worked hard to fight liquor addiction in her own community and in this connection has travelled widely in India.
83. V.L. Pandit, *The Scope of Happiness*, p. 150. See also Chapter 7, below.
84. S. Nagar 'Contribution of Women of Allahabad'.
85. Rameshwari Nehru Papers, E. No. 6, p. 3.
86. V.L. Pandit, *The Scope of Happiness*, p. 163.
87. Ibid., p. 164.
88. Krishna Hutheesing, *Jail Ke Ve Din*. Kashi (Varanasi): Mudran Gyan Mandal Yantralaya Limited, Kashi, 1944, p. 56.
89. Ibid., p. 61.

90. Ibid., p. 70.
91. Interview with Late Kalavati Misra at her residence in Kydganj in February 1996. After coming out of prison Kalavati's social and political activities continued. She taught children in the Harijan colonies, arranged for their books and also for milk for the women who were pregnant. She taught spinning on the 'ambar' charkha to 200 women and meanwhile continued her own studies with the support of Indira Gandhi. She was able to complete the teacher's training course and became a primary school teacher in 1948 and later in 1950 became the Principal of the primary section. She was also active in the local office of the Mahila Congress in Kydganj where she conducted discussions among the women.
92. Information obtained during interview with Raj Rani Nishad; also, K. Hutheesing, *Jail Ke Ve Din*, p. 195.
93. K. Hutheesing, *Jail Ke Ve Din*, p. 96.
94. Ibid., p. 100.
95. V.L. Pandit, *The Scope of Happiness*, p. 164.
96. Letter to Jawaharlal Nehru, 7 May 1941. Jawaharlal Nehru (ed.), *A Bunch of Old Letters: Being Mostly Written to Jawaharlal Nehru and Some Written by Him* (New Edition, with an Introduction by Sunil Khilnani). New Delhi: Penguin/Viking, 2005, p. 461.
97. K. Hutheesing, *With No Regrets*, p. 88.
98. V.L. Pandit, *The Scope of Happiness*, p. 164.
99. Interview with Late Mrs Kamla Bahuguna at her residence on Hastings Road (now Nyaya Marg) in November 1996. Mrs Bahuguna informed the author that her mother Sukhraj defied her husband who was an eminent Professor of the Department of History, University of Allahabad, to join the Civil Disobedience movements of 1930 and 1932. As a child Mrs Kamla Bahuguna (then Tripathi) was also active in the *Vanar Sena* or Monkey Brigade, headed by Indira Nehru. After her marriage to Late Mr Hemwati Nandan Bahuguna, she had a very active political career.
100. Interview with Mrs Pratibha Malaviya.
101. Pandit, *The Scope of Happiness*, p. 171.

Chapter 4

Conservatives Become Radicals in Lucknow

After the turbulent days of the Revolt of 1857 the feudal ethos of Lucknow regained its strength, not least on account of the 'Oudh Policy' designed to foster unflinching loyalty to the Raj in return for the preservation of the privileges and primacy of the landed elites.[1] A notable characteristic of this ethos was that women were not to be found in any public activity. It was the Home Rule Movement in the years 1916 and 1917, under the leadership of Mrs Annie Besant and Bal Gangadhar Tilak, which brought about political mobilization of women of the educated classes to a considerable extent. As in Allahabad, the arrest of Mrs Annie Besant in June 1917 provoked special 'ladies meetings' in Lucknow as well, for expressing solidarity with Annie Besant; most meetings appear to be well attended.[2] These were afternoon meetings in which women were exhorted to join the Home Rule League in large numbers.

To further the cause of Home Rule it was decided that a special UP Provincial Congress would be held in Lucknow on 10 August 1917. Delegates to this Congress were chosen from each district, and an effort was made to elect women as delegates as well. Delegates came from as far as Delhi and Ajmer-Merwara, and several resolutions were passed, including one that was critical of the continued internment of the Ali brothers.[3] Evidence of women's own political initiative was still lacking.

A major surge in women's mobilization in the UP was evident as a result of the Non-Cooperation Movement under Mahatma Gandhi's leadership. In a speech at Lucknow on 5 October 1920, Gandhi compared the British Empire to Satan and told his audience that it was the duty of every Indian to destroy it. In bold language he said that Indians could have no relations with the British government until it had 'not only restored our wealth' but 'also given us back our honour and freedom'.[4] On 11 January 1922, a women's meeting was held in Lucknow in defiance of prohibitory orders. According to newspaper reports there were 'several Muhammadan ladies present' as also Mrs Krishna Lal Nehru, the daughter of the Minister for Local Self-Government. The meeting was however presided over by a male, Abdul Qari. The women were exhorted to use hand-made *khaddar* and to 'encourage the men to join the national movement'.[5]

It was the organized boycott of the visit of the Simon Commission to Lucknow that brought the women out on the streets of the city. The appointment of the all-White Simon Commission to decide constitutional changes for India incensed Indians across the political spectrum, and there was a near-unanimous decision to boycott his visit on 30 November 1928. From 28 November, Jawaharlal Nehru and Govind Ballabh Pant organized meetings and processions to spread the message of boycott. On the 29 November, the procession was violently attacked by the police and many received injuries from *lathi* blows, including Jawaharlal Nehru and Govind Ballabh Pant. A huge meeting was called the same evening in Aminuddaulah Park to condemn the police action.[6]

Fully aware of the risks involved, women joined the procession on 30 November, the day Simon was to arrive in Lucknow.

Mrs Suniti Mitra, who had earlier been arrested in Bengal during the Non-Cooperation Movement, carried the tri-colour national flag and led the women. The procession marched peacefully from Aminabad via Latouche Road and reached Charbagh Railway Station just before Simon was to arrive at 7 a.m., all the while shouting the slogan 'Simon, go back'. The army and police battalions ordered the demonstrators to disperse, but this was stoutly opposed. *Lathi* charge was ordered and the horse-mounted police also charged ahead to disperse the crowds; the demonstrators were trampled upon and suffered serious injuries. The injured included several women, like Mrs Suniti Devi Mitra and Mrs Dhanraj Bakshi.[7]

It was participation in the Simon agitation that gave a real fillip to the formation of Youth Leagues and associations all over the country. The UP Youth Conference was organized in Lucknow by the UP Youth League on 15 and 16 September 1929. Mrs Sarojini Naidu presided over the conference, which was attended by many public representatives including several women. A condolence resolution was passed to mourn the recent death of Jatindranath Das in Lahore jail after 63 days of hunger strike in a bid to better jail conditions for political prisoners. Death of revolutionaries like Jatin Das and Khudiram Bose and nationalists like Lala Lajpat Rai convinced many women of the tyrannical nature of the British regime.[8]

The salt *satyagraha* begun by Mahatma Gandhi in April 1930 elicited an enthusiastic response from women volunteers in Lucknow. Over 300 women attended a meeting at 4 p.m. on 23 April 1930 at the Zenana Park in Lucknow where they prepared 78 packets of contraband salt which were sold for 1 anna each. Among the speakers at the meeting were Mrs Suniti Devi Mitra, Smt Kanti Devi Awasthi and Mrs Dhanraj Bakshi. Mrs Bakshi presided over the meeting.[9]

In April 1930, women's mobilization was rapid across the United Provinces, organized partly through big meetings as in Kanpur, Allahabad, Firozabad, Benaras and Lucknow. Picketing of shops selling foreign cloth was begun on a campaign footing almost at the same time as the making of contraband salt. It started on 25 April 1930 with volunteers asking shopkeepers in Aminabad to give a written undertaking to isolate foreign cloth. Over a dozen shopkeepers accepted the advice of Congress volunteers and their customers returned the cloth that they had bought. At Chowk Bazar also, volunteers undertook picketing of shops selling foreign cloth at four places. Mrs Suniti Devi Mitra led the women volunteers.[10] Suniti Mitra and one Mrs Sharma also succeeded in persuading some Muslim men to exchange their foreign *fez* caps for *khaddar* Gandhi caps.[11]

The British Government had placed many restrictions on the taking out of processions. On 25 May 1930, in Lucknow, women joined the long procession going to Hazratganj. The police ordered the leader of the procession Mrs Suniti Mitra to take a different route. On her refusal she was arrested and *lathis* rained down on the processionists. The women were taken two miles outside the city and left to fend for themselves.[12] As yet punishments were not hard, but on 30 May, Mrs Mitra was arrested with a band of *satyagrahis* for violating Section 144 and sentenced to a six-month imprisonment.[13]

As repression increased with new Ordinances coming into force, the momentum of *satyagraha* grew correspondingly and going to jail became a matter of honour. Women often led the volunteer groups called *jathas*. Mrs Kanti Devi Awasthi led the ninth *jatha* and was arrested on 13 June 1930 for violating Section 144. On 24 November, Mrs Neeru Devi of Aminabad, Mrs Rama Devi, Shivrani Devi and Raju Devi, all of Ganeshganj, were sentenced to six weeks in prison under Ordinances 4 and 5.[14] Shivrani Devi was the wife of the celebrated writer Premchand, who recorded the

Kanti Devi Awasthi

deep impact of her arrest and imprisonment on him in the following words:

> I saw her yesterday in prison and found her cheerful as ever. She has left us all behind and I now appear smaller in my own eyes. She has gone up a hundred fold in my esteem. But until she comes and relieves me, I shall have to bear the burden of running the household.[15]

Women from the most populous *mohallas* came out in full strength. Apart from prison sentences, heavy fines were imposed and refusal to pay (which was Congress policy) meant many more days in prison. On 19 January 1931, Mrs Ram Dulari Devi of Aminabad, Mrs Shyamrani Sahni of Golaganj and Mrs Saraswati Devi from the Congress office were sentenced to six months in prison and fines ranging from Rs. 10 to 200 were imposed on them. Motivation was so high at the time that many of the women activists repeatedly went to prison. Among these were Mrs Suniti Mitra, Mrs Kanti Devi Awasthi, Mrs Annapurna Devi, Dulari Devi and Shyamrani Sahni.

Gandhi's arrest on 5 January 1932 was the signal for the most brutal repression of the movement. All civil rights were suspended. Property was confiscated up to the value of the fine if it was not paid. But this did not deter the women. Although Section 144 IPC was clamped on the city, a strike was observed on 6 January 1932, and big meetings were held in defiance of Section 144. Mrs Suniti Mitra had been appointed a member of the 'Council of Action' and for her participation in a meeting she was arrested with others on 6 January 1932. She was given a sentence of three months rigorous imprisonment and a fine of Rs. 200 was imposed on her, in default of which she served a further one-and-a-half months in prison.[16] Annapurna Devi was also arrested on 6 January for addressing a gathering at Aminabad Park. She received a sentence of one month rigorous imprisonment and a fine of Rs. 200 in default of which she served another one and a half months in prison like Mrs Mitra.[17] On 9 January 1932, 4 more women along

Vijayalakshmi Pandit Hoisting National Flag at Mahila Vidyalaya (1936), Lucknow

Congress Women Volunteers welcoming Jawaharlal Nehru at Lucknow 1936

with 13 male volunteers were arrested for defying Section 144.[18] More arrests followed on 13 January 1932. [19]

In fact, to make the picketing more effective, women began to join the men in lying down in front of the shops selling foreign goods and liquor. This method of *satyagraha* was most visible in Aminabad, Nakhas, Chowk and Hazratganj, which were the main shopping markets.[20] Arrests followed, and Mrs Ganga Devi (Saadatganj), Ram Dulari Devi (Ganeshganj), Sundar Devi and Rama Devi Tandon were sent to prison for varying terms. Congress 'dictators', that is those in charge of local Civil Disobedience activities, were often women. On 15 January 1933, many of the provincial dictators who had congregated in Lucknow to hoist the national flag in Aminuddaulah Park were arrested, and those included two women. An important contribution of women volunteers to the struggle for freedom was the care they provided for the families of political prisoners who were often left destitute.[21]

A major difference between the two mass movements, that is Non-Cooperation and Civil Disobedience in the United Provinces, was the absence of well-known Muslim women in the latter movement. This was really a reflection of the worsening communal situation in the country since 1924 when a spate of riots began and continued to occur not only in the UP but across North-Western, Northern and Eastern parts of the country till 1927. No less than 91 communal outbreaks were recorded in UP alone.[22]

Constructive activities occupied the national workers in the years intervening between Civil Disobedience of 1930–1933 and the individual *Satyagraha Movement* of 1940–1941. Gandhi's visits to Lucknow, first in 1934, and again in 1935 for the Golden Jubilee celebrations of the Indian National Congress, added to the enthusiasm. *Prabhat pheris*, singing of national songs, flag-hoisting and big public meetings became a daily affair. Craft exhibitions were an important part of political gatherings with a view to promoting economic self-sufficiency of the nation.

Women contributed in no small way to the success of the All-India Congress Session, which took place in Lucknow in 1936.

Mrs Suniti Mitra was appointed captain of the women volunteers while Mrs Godavari Bhargava, Mrs Dhanraj Bakshi and Mrs Kanti Devi Awasthi were among the chief organizers. For the first time, an All-India *Qaumi Mushaira* was held as part of the Congress Session, at which poets and singers from different parts of the country rendered patriotic compositions.[23]

The popular impact of the Civil Disobedience Movement was demonstrated when the results of the elections in the provinces were announced in early 1937. The Congress was able to form ministries in 8 out of 11 provinces. In the elections to the Legislative Assembly of the United Provinces in 1937 two women from Lucknow were elected. They were Begum Habibullah of the Muslim League and Mrs Suniti Devi Mitra of the Congress while more were elected from the rest of the United Provinces on Congress tickets. All gave a good account of themselves in the deliberations of the Assembly.[24] This subject is dealt with in Chapter 7. Suniti Devi Mitra won from an unreserved seat in Rae Bareli district on a Congress ticket by defeating a well-known *taluqdar*, the Raja of Tiloi, by an impressive margin.[25]

Suniti Devi Mitra demonstrated her strong gender sensitivity in an interesting argument in the Legislative Assembly when the qualifications of those eligible to be appointed as Honorary Magistrates were being discussed. Dr Kailash Nath Katju, the Minister of Justice, had moved that the minimum age for women should be higher than that for men as they were light-hearted! Suniti Devi Mitra countered this argument and maintained that women acquired mental maturity much earlier than men. Therefore, it would be better to have a lower age qualification for women than for men. She also argued that there ought to be a later retirement age for women, since they continued to be alert even after the age of 50, whereas men would begin to lose their mental faculties by this time.[26] (A more exhaustive discussion on this episode follows in Chapter 7.)

Begum Habibullah of the Muslim League was also vocal on several issues in the Assembly discussions. Her perspective was different from that of Uma Nehru of the Congress, who desired that all Indians should be united in their support for the proposed Constituent Assembly.[27] Begum Habibullah, like other Muslim League members, wanted guarantees for minorities saying that the wishes of 10 crore Muslims could not be ignored. Past experience, she said, had shown that the greater the emphasis placed on unanimity the more the side-lining of the minorities occurred.[28]

In the course of the discussion on the 1939 budget, Begum Habibullah complained that the government had not made adequate provision for female education, especially for Muslim girls.[29] This in reality was contrary to the Report of the United Provinces Primary and Secondary Education Reorganisation Committee, prepared in 1939, which spoke of 'rapid progress of girls' education'. The Report largely drew upon Mahatma Gandhi's ideas on Basic Education which was opposed to any distinction based on sex in the matter of co-education for children, especially until the age of 10. Muslim League members held a different opinion on this issue of common education.

The Individual Satyagraha campaign of 1940–1941 brought the women out again, in large numbers. Going to jail became a matter of prestige; several women went twice within 12 months. Between December 1940 and October 1941 more than 20 women were arrested in Lucknow for Individual *Satyagraha*, and four of these were from rural areas. They were sentenced to prison for terms varying between three months and six months with fines from Rs. 15 to Rs. 100. Several of them broke the law again and were rearrested. Shanta Devi Vaidya was first arrested in December 1940 and given a prison term for six months[30] and again in November 1941 a prison term for three months. Tara Rani, 'dictator' of the Provincial Congress Committee, Lucknow, did her first term in January 1941 for three months, then again for six months in October 1941. Ram Dulari Devi who had been to jail twice during the Civil Disobedience Movement did two more jail terms during the Individual Satyagraha campaign.[31] All these women went to jail again, some for the fourth or fifth time, during the *Quit India* Movement between 1942 and 1943.[32]

That women were fully aware of the political issues involved in the Individual *Satyagraha* of 1940–1941 is obvious from the heroic statement of Mrs Kanti Devi Awasthi before the City Magistrate of Lucknow at the time of her conviction. She said that she had only done her duty as a true worker of the Indian National Congress. If despite this she was considered a law breaker, she would proudly suffer the maximum punishment. Moreover, she said, any defence offered would be useless as in the present case the prosecutor was also the judge. She concluded by thanking the official for giving her a patient hearing.[33]

The Individual *Satyagraha* campaign struck deep roots in the villages in Lucknow district due mainly to the efforts of women volunteers. Many of these villages were inhabited by the Harijan community, yet they joined the demonstrations and processions in large numbers. On 10 January 1941, Mrs Shivrajvati Nehru offered *satyagraha* in Gauri village, but as she was not arrested she began touring other villages. First she went to Berbenda Khera where she was joined by 200 *kisans*,[34] then to Sakera by which time the crowd had swelled to 2,000 villagers. From there she proceeded to Sakai Khera, Balera, Madarikhera, Kathingara, Bhavani Khera and Gurudeen Khera and at each village she shouted antiwar slogans and repeated the message of Mahatma Gandhi regarding the Second World War. At Kakori Bazaar a huge gathering waited to listen to her, and, on her way back to Lucknow, she stopped over at the Kakori police station, where 150 *kisans* were waiting to see her and asked her for Gandhi's message. At 3.30 p.m. on 11 January she reached Lucknow where she was arrested immediately upon arrival. She was given three months simple imprisonment.[35]

On 20 February 1941, 300 women and students marched in a joint procession from the Kisan Library in Kakori village. As they went around the village they were joined by thousands of villagers. Rajrani Devi (60 years of age), Mohini Devi (65 years) and Savitri Devi were all arrested for shouting anti-War slogans and delivering anti-War speeches. They presented handbills to the policemen who came to arrest them. All three ladies were charged with a fine of Rs. 15, and given three months simple imprisonment.[36]

Women were not in the background even during the *Quit India* Movement of 1942 in spite of its revolutionary nature. In Lucknow, as in the rest of the country, all Congress Committees and offices were declared unlawful and so were public meetings and processions (from 9 August 1942). Despite this, crowds and processions continued to protest against the sudden arrest of all Congress leaders, and Gandhi's message of *Do or Die* was raised everywhere. On 10 August, government properties like railway stations and post offices were attacked and set on fire. It was in these circumstances that students of Lucknow University, including many girls, started a procession towards the city, but when they reached the Monkey Bridge the police posted there resorted to indiscriminate firing and many were injured as a result. The students declared a strike in Lucknow University, which was followed by strikes in many colleges. Mrs Shivrajvati Nehru organized the strike in Mahila College and soon after hoisted the National Flag in Jhandewala Park. The police took the flag down and threw it away. Immediately the crowd standing there picked it up and tried to restore it, but all were arrested. Shivrajvati Nehru was put under house arrest.[37]

Among the unlawful activities being performed by women activists at the time were the distribution of proscribed nationalist literature, delivering anti-War speeches, participating in demonstrations and hoisting the national flag in public places. All these led to arrests and prosecution.[38] Mrs Ramdev Azad was given rigorous imprisonment for one year on 15 August 1942 and a fine of Rs. 50. Mrs Ram Dulari Devi was sentenced to prison for nine months on 9 December 1942. Asha Lata Shukla, Shanta Devi Vaidya, Swaroop Kumari Bakshi, Surjit Kaur, Lakshmi Devi, Rama Devi and Kanti Devi Awasthi were all put under house arrest. Mrs S.N. Tagore and Ms Purushottam were arrested on Faizabad Road for distributing anti-War pamphlets on 22 October 1942.[39]

Thus, contrary to the general impression, there is ample evidence to establish that women in Lucknow from all classes and backgrounds were not only participating actively but were often leading the movement for the freedom of the country.

NOTES

1. For analytical perspectives on the 'Oudh Policy' and its social and political determinants, see Thomas R. Metcalf, *The Aftermath of Revolt, India 1857–1870* (Princeton University Press, 1964), pp. 134–138; Veena Talwar Oldenberg, *The Making of Colonial Lucknow, 1856–1877* (Princeton University Press, 1984), pp. 199–212, 243–245.
2. *The Leader*, 10 August 1917, p. 6
3. *The Leader*, 13 August 1917, p. 6 and 17 August 1917, p. 7.
4. *Navajivan* (Gujarati), 31 October 1920; *CWMG* Vol. 18, pp. 350–351.
5. *The Leader*, 28 January 1922, p. 6.
6. Tabassum Nizami Bhartiya, *Lucknow Janpad ka Rashtriya Itihas.* Lucknow: Uttar Pradesh Sahitya Sadan, 1961, p. 140 (available at the UP State Archives, Lucknow).
7. Based on interview in April 1997 at Lucknow, with Mrs Swaroop Kumari Bakshi, daughter-in-law of Lucknow freedom fighter Dhanraj Bakshi and herself a freedom fighter and former Cabinet Minister for Education, Uttar Pradesh.
8. Ibid.
9. *The Leader*, Allahabad, Thursday, 24 April 1930.
10. *The Leader*, Allahabad, Thursday, 1 May 1930.
11. *The Leader*, 4 May 1930, p. 10.
12. *The Leader*, Allahabad, Monday, 26 May 1930.
13. T.N. Bhartiya, *Lucknow Janpad ka Rashtriya Itihas*, p. 157.

14. Ibid., p. 176.
15. Amrit Rai, *Premchand: A Life*, trans. Harish Trivedi. New Delhi: Oxford University Press, 1982, p. 260.
16. *The Leader*, Allahabad, January 7, 1932.
17. *The Leader*, Allahabad, January 9, 1932.
18. *The Leader*, Allahabad, 9 January 1932.
19. *The Leader*, Allahabad, 11 January 1932.
20. Based on interview with Miss Cecilia Phillips, former Director of Women's Education, UP, then student of Lucknow University (May 1997).
21. Based on interviews with Mrs Swaroop Kumari Bakshi; Pratibha Malaviya, daughter of Mrs Ketaki Bhatt, freedom fighter of Allahabad; and Mrs Kamala Bahuguna, an activist of Allahabad and wife of Hemwati Nandan Bahuguna, former Chief Minister of UP.
22. Sumit Sarkar, *Modern India*, 1885–1947. Delhi: MacMillan, 2004, p. 233.
23. T.N. Bhartiya, *Lucknow Janpad ka Rashtriya Itihas*, pp. 224–229.
24. Proceedings of the UP Legislative Assembly Library (hereinafter, UPLAP) of the Vidhan Sabha, Lucknow, and Central Library, Benaras Hindu University, Varanasi.
25. P.D. Reeves, B.D. Graham and J.M. Goodman, *Handbook to Elections in Uttar Pradesh, 1920–1951* (New Delhi: Manohar, 1975), p. 307.
26. Speech on 1 February 1938, UPLAP, p. 1304, *Discussion on Rules Regarding Appointment of Honorary Magistrates.*
27. *UPLAP*, Vol. 1, p. 278; discussion on 6 September 1937.
28. *UPLAP*, Vol. 1, pp. 279–281.
29. Discussion on 14 March 1939, N.N. Mitra, *Indian Annual Register, 1939, Vol. 1*, January–June 1939, pp. 220–221.
30. *National Herald*, Lucknow, 4 December 1940 and *The Leader*, Allahabad, 7 December 1940.
31. *National Herald*, Lucknow, January 25, 1941.
32. T.N. Bhartiya, *Lucknow Janpad ka Rashtriya Itihas*, pp. 243–252.

33. *Aaj*, Varanasi, 30 January 1941.
34. Peasants.
35. Meera Devi, 'Gandhi Ka Aahvaan: Lucknow Janpad Ki Mahilayen (1940-41)', in Vinaya Chandra Pande and Sunit Singh (eds), *Swatantrata Andolan Evam Uttar Pradesh*. New Delhi: APH Publishing Corporation, 2000, pp. 212–216.
36. Ibid.
37. T.N. Bhartiya, *Lucknow Janpad ka Rashtriya Itihas*, pp. 286–290.
38. Based on interview with Mrs Swaroop Kumari Bakshi.
39. T.N. Bhartiya, *Lucknow Janpad ka Rashtriya Itihas*, pp. 255–257.

Chapter 5

Agra Women Storm Male Bastions

Agra was unique in the United Provinces in the sense that the level of women's mobilization during the national struggle for freedom was much greater than in other places. The women activists often belonged to families which had been involved in the national movement since its inception. Vernacular education of a primary or higher standard, and in some cases college education, was also a common factor, though in the movement of 1930 and 1932, many women, barely educated, were found to be highly motivated in the national cause.

Mahatma Gandhi visited Agra in November 1920 to propagate the cause of non-cooperation. At two public meetings he advocated the boycott of courts, councils, schools and foreign goods, particularly foreign cloth. At a meeting of students, he said, 'You may leave college only if the cruel injustice done to the country and to the Muslims has kindled a fire in your hearts.'[1]

Undeniably, the pioneer and sustainer of the women's political movement in Agra during the nationalist phase was Parvati Devi.

She was born in 1887 in Baluchistan and brought up there. She was married to a doctor but was widowed within two-and-a-half years and left with a baby daughter. For livelihood, she took up the job of headmistress of Vedic Dharma Balika Pathshala in Amritsar but resigned after Mahatma Gandhi's call for non-cooperation. Amritsar was perhaps the most deeply impacted place in India after the Jallianwala Bagh massacre there on 13 April 1919. She worked at the *Swaraj Ashram* of Dr Saifuddin Kitchlew at Amritsar, where she met Mahatma Gandhi. Thereafter, she became an active member of the Punjab Congress Committee and began touring and propagating the national cause.[2]

A turning point came when Parvati Devi was arrested and sent to prison for her anti-British speeches delivered in Meerut and Hapur. On 19 November 1922, she was awarded two years rigorous imprisonment which she suffered in Lahore jail, the longest term awarded to any woman in the movement until then and the only woman to have earned the distinction in the United Provinces or Punjab. *The Leader* gave prominence to the news, particularly the harsh manner of her arrest and the severity of her punishment.[3] It also highlighted 'her spirited reply in her defence', which 'is indeed an inspiring one and ought to make most "men" ashamed of their existence.'[4] Her arrest and punishment deeply affected the people of Meerut and Muzaffarnagar, so much so that in the latter town a meeting was organized in her honour at the Town Hall, even against the wishes of the Chairman of the Municipal Board. The crowd was so large that tickets had to be issued to a limited number of persons.[5]

A factor which did galvanize women in Agra to join the national struggle was the visit of Mahatma Gandhi in September 1929. Gandhi came to Agra as part of his tour of the United Provinces to prepare the country for Civil Disobedience after the expiry of the ultimatum of 31 December 1929. His mission was to collect donations for the *khadi* work and advocacy for the AICC programme of non-cooperation. This also underlined 'the triple constructive programme, *viz.* the boycott of foreign cloth through *khadi*, the

Moola Devi

suppression of the drink and drug evil and the elimination of untouchability by the Hindus'. 'Such a programme needed a vast army of volunteers,' he said; hence, the reorganization of the Congress and enrolment of new members was a necessity.

Gandhi's austerity and need for transparency was such that he refused addresses of honour that were framed saying that he did not have the space to keep them; second, 'every rupee spent in framing meant the loss of one woman's subsistence for sixteen days.' He said that he meant no disrespect by desiring to auction them as he had done so before and one address in Andhra fetched 10,000 rupees.[6] At the end of his speech he said, 'Let me warn you solemnly that if we do nothing now, *swaraj* or independence *is* not going to drop down from heaven by a mere declaration by the Congress in December. I will go further and say that unless in the mean time we shall have forged an effective sanction to back our declaration which we want to make, if the Government should refuse to accept by the midnight of 31 December 1929 the national demand, our declaration will remain a dead letter and we shall be unable to do anything effective during 1930.' Even young girls like Champawati, a mere 13-year-old, and Damayanti Devi Chaturvedi acknowledged the deep impact left by him which filled them with love for their country and the desire to make sacrifices for her liberation. Other women like Moola Devi, Poornima Devi, Bhagwati Devi Paliwal and Satyawati Rawat stayed with their husbands in Sevagram or Wardha in close proximity to Gandhi and found their experiences inspiring.[7]

Parvati Devi, mentioned earlier, came to Agra, where her daughter lived, in 1930, and immediately set up a National Women's Committee and began door-to-door visits to motivate women to join the national movement. On 23 April 1930, during the salt *satyagraha* at Runakta, the police forcibly seized huge quantities of salt, implements and personal belongings of the volunteers, and many were injured when they resisted. On the 24 April, volunteers from Runakta came to the Kotwali in Agra and sat on *dharna* at the entrance to the Kotwali. Women volunteers of Agra joined the picketing by lying down on the ground. Their demand was the return of the seized goods. This crowd was assaulted by the police and were dragged out and thrown on the road. They managed to get back again only to be treated the same way. Many women received serious injuries. Among them were Parvati Devi, Sukh Devi Paliwal, Shiva Devi Dikshit and Draupadi Devi Sharma.[8] Ultimately the authorities had to return the goods that had been seized in Runakta. Some of the other women volunteers in this *satyagraha* were Vidyadhari Jauhari,[9] Angoori Devi Jain, Satyawati Rawat, Anandi Devi and Damayanti Devi Chaturvedi.[10]

Shiva Devi Dikshit

Draupadi Devi Sharma

A significant achievement by a group of 35 women volunteers was the signed pledge obtained from over 150 cloth merchants of Agra in April 1930 that they would not sell imported cloth for six months. Some *bajaj* merchants (clothiers) refused to sign the pledge; as a result their shops were picketed and finally they too joined the others. The results became obvious soon. On 19 May 1930, Motilal Nehru announced that Agra was the first place in India to put a seal on the sale of foreign cloth. The campaign to obtain the pledge was led by Parvati Devi, Sukh Devi Paliwal and Damayanti Devi Chaturvedi.[11]

Angoori Devi Jain

The boycott of foreign cloth was propagated as a weapon to weaken the foreign government and the use of *swadeshi* cloth, that is, *khadi* and plying the *charkha*, that is, the spinning wheel were advocated by the women volunteers as means to strengthen the nation. Their strategy was to move from village to village, holding small meetings explaining these issues. Mohini Devi Singhal, Premwati Misra, Urmila Devi, Saraswati Devi, Draupadi Devi Sharma, Satyawati Rawat and Bhagwati Devi Paliwal were all deeply involved in this work. Bhagwati Devi, in the course of her interview mentioned the villages, namely, Khandauli, Dhanauli, Achnera and Malpura, where they would visit and urge the women to perform *satyagraha,* like picketing government schools or toll offices and seek imprisonment. In the city of Agra, Bhagwati Devi said that women activists would collect Khadi cloth and *charkhas* from the *Khadi* Ashram in Rajamandi and would then visit different *mohallas* like Jauhari Bazaar, Rawatpara, Belanganj, Sadar Bazaar and smaller *bastis* where they would teach the women to ply the charkha and urge them to buy *khadi* cloth.[12]

Women were active supporters of the flag *satyagraha* at Kirawali in August 1930. This had been launched for the return of flags and other things confiscated from the volunteers. The police acted in a barbaric manner and it was mainly to highlight this that a team led by Vidyawati Rathor and Vidyadhari Jauhari broke the tight cordon of mounted police and managed to reach the *tehsil* headquarters at Kirawali. Vidyawati Rathor was arrested. The *satyagraha* ended on 21 August with the return of ambulance equipment, flags and a cot.[13]

Three young girls, who happened to be sisters, also created history in Kirawali. They were Champawati, Chandrakali and Asharfi Devi, aged 13, 11 and 9 years, respectively. They were daughters of Thakur Bhanwar Singh. The three had a unique style of propagating the message of national struggle. Moving from village to village, singing national songs, they would carry bangles and inform the people that if they were not in the struggle to free the country they should wear bangles to proclaim their cowardice. In the campaigns of 1930 and 1932, Champawati was sent to prison for six months and three months, respectively. Her two younger sisters were also in prison during the no-tax campaign of 1932.[14]

Picketing of liquor shops was also an important activity from the beginning of the Civil Disobedience campaign. Women volunteers were in the forefront here too, even though it involved humiliating treatment by the police. None of the volunteers physically resisted even under the greatest provocation.[15] A campaign shouldered almost exclusively by the women was that of mobilizing students to boycott government schools and colleges, which were described as 'denationalizing institutions'. Women would lead processions to the selected institutions, picket their entrance, sing national songs, distribute handbills and ask the students to leave the institution and join national institutions.[16] Parvati Devi was arrested and sent to prison for picketing Agra and St. John's Colleges on 28 July 1930.[17] Mrs Sukh Devi Paliwal was arrested while addressing the students of Agra College.[18] Vidyadhari Jauhari, headmistress of Indra Bhan Girls School, and another senior teacher, Champa Devi, were suspended by the management for their nationalist activities. Immediately, a forceful demonstration was made by women volunteers outside the school, as a result of which the suspension order was revoked.[19]

A significant event which received wide publicity was the observance of 'Boycott Week' by the Congress in Agra, from 19 August to 26 August 1930. Each day of the week was celebrated to highlight a special purpose. Thus, there was a Flag-Hoisting Day, *Khadi* Day, Ladies Day, Anti-Liquor Day, Children's Day, Patriots Day and Students Day. The Flag-Hoisting Day began with a huge procession of 4,000 men and women who marched to Nayaganj where Mrs Vidyadhari Jauhari unfurled the National Flag on the municipal building. In her speech she outlined the plans for the Boycott Week and congratulated the volunteers of Kirawali for the successful outcome of their *satyagraha*. On *Khadi* Day, every one wore *khadi* and propagated its cause in the main bazaar. A *charkha* and *takli* competition was also held on that day.[20]

The Dayalbagh *dharna* of September 1930 is remembered for the valiant resistance put up by women volunteers against the mindless violence of the police. An attempt was made to trample them with horses and motorcars; they were assaulted with whips and *lathis*, but they carried on their *satyagraha* undaunted. Parvati Devi, Anandi Devi, Sukh Devi Paliwal, Angoori Devi Jain were among the many women who actively participated in this demonstration. Bhagyawati Devi who was the 'dictator' of the local Congress unit at that time received serious injuries.[21]

Another example of their heroic powers of endurance was their role in the no-tax agitation in Agra district. Barauda village was the centre of this agitation, and it had been prepared like Bardoli in Gujarat. Women volunteers walked 12 miles from the city to reach Barauda in order to participate in the *satyagraha*. But the government unleashed violence even before it started. Many women received injuries as they were trampled by horses. Among them were Angoori Devi Jain, Champa Devi, Parvati Devi and Anandi Devi.[22] Vidyadhari Jauhari and other women rendered medical help to many who were seriously injured in this campaign.[23]

Firozabad, then part of Agra district, was the storm centre of women's agitation from 1930. The Dwarkadheesh temple was chosen to break the untouchability law which prohibited Harijans from entering the temple precincts. In 1930 the *satyagraha* was led by Sukhdevi Paliwal and Premvati Misra (then Sharma). Sukh Devi was arrested but later released. In 1932 these women volunteers urged the owners of temples to use *khadi* cloth for the deities and hoist national flags. They generally received a good response and many temples put up signboards saying that only those wearing *khadi* could enter them. Seth Kanhaiya Lal, one of the temple owners, refused to comply with any of the requests with the result that women volunteers began a demonstration at the entrance to the temple. Thousands of people came to witness the scene. Seth Kanhaiya Lal reported the matter to the police and Sukh Devi Paliwal was arrested. Immediately other women took her place and public enthusiasm rose perceptibly. National slogans were shouted and the *satyagraha* went on for several days during which Satyawati Rawat, Champawati, Draupadi Devi, Ummodibai, Kripa Devi, Nanhi Devi, Triveni Devi, Saraswati Devi, Gulab Devi, Ramkali and Tikawati Devi were all arrested.

Meanwhile a social boycott of Seth Kanhaiya Lal took place with the result that he withdrew his complaint and left Firozabad. The national flag was unfurled on the temple tower. As the number of women volunteers in jail kept swelling, the District Magistrate was more or less compelled to release all of them. As soon as these ladies reached Firozabad they were received like heroines and thousands joined in the ovation. Flowers and expensive necklaces were showered on them. There was a public meeting in which Sukh Devi and Angoori Devi gave speeches.[24] The temple *satyagraha* in Firozabad heightened national and social consciousness. Sukh Devi Paliwal continued her work there. She was arrested on 10 October 1932 and sentenced to six months in prison. Among the other active volunteers in Firozabad were Kabuli Devi, Triveni Devi, Radhabai, Champavati and Premvati.[25]

Saraswati Devi Paliwal

Agra was outstanding in the United Provinces for its successful movement against foreign cloth. Almost all merchants, partly because of the fear of picketing and the general hostility that prevailed towards imported goods, refused to sell or stock foreign cloth or goods. There was a demand only for Indian articles.[26]

The issues of women's oppression and their lowly status were also raised frequently by the women volunteers in their speeches. Problems of *purdah*, dowry system, child marriage, untouchability and financial dependence were discussed in meetings by women like Premvati Misra, Damayanti Devi Chaturvedi, Sukh Devi Paliwal, Draupadi Devi Sharma, Vidyawati Rathor, Angoori Devi and Saraswati Devi.[27]

The hardships of prison life were suffered not only by the women volunteers but quite often by their young children also. Satyawati Rawat was given five months rigorous imprisonment in April 1931. She went to jail with her five-month-old daughter. In 1932 she again went to prison for 11 months, but this time her daughter remained with friends.[28] Saraswati Devi went to prison in 1932 with her six-month-old son. Sukh Devi Paliwal and Parvati Devi went to prison innumerable times. In fact, Sukh Devi used to say that going to jail was like going to her *maika* (parental home)![29]

After the calling off of the Civil Disobedience Movement in 1934 by Mahatma Gandhi, women volunteers in Agra as elsewhere engaged in constructive activities as conceptualized by Gandhi. This involved village-uplift programmes, including anti-untouchability work, mobilizing women to join the *charkha* movement and involving them in *satyagraha*.[30]

In the provincial elections for legislative assemblies held in the winter of 1936–1937, Agra's Vidyawati Rathor was among the nine successful women who won on Congress ticket. She stood from an unreserved rural seat, Etah District South, and defeated C.Y. Chintamani, the well-known journalist and editor of *The Leader*![31] In the Legislative Assembly she spoke on matters relating to provincial excise and prohibition.[32] She was also a member of the UP Consolidation of Holdings Committee. Like other Congress male legislators, Vidyawati Rathor was active in mass mobilization in the United Provinces, participating in political conferences, Kisan meetings, students' conferences and demonstrations. Though not a legislator, Parvati Devi was also involved in these activities as President of the Agra District Kisan Sabha in 1937.[33]

By 1939–1940, after the outbreak of Second World War, national politics had again reached a stage where a mass movement for the final liberation of the country was being anticipated. This atmosphere of national resurgence was palpable even among the young daughters of activists. Saroj Rawat, who was only 10 years old and a student of Class V in Kanya Pathshala, Singigili, in 1940, was fully aware of the struggle for national freedom. She attended political meetings with her father, Jagan Prasad Rawat, in rural areas and often led the singing of national songs such as *Vande Mataram* and *Jhanda Uncha Rahe Hamara*. She would regularly participate in *prabhat pheris* and carry messages of volunteers; she and two other girls would often gather the village children and teach them to raise slogans that were popular in the national movement.[34]

Satyawati Paliwal

Satyawati Paliwal, a 10-year-old in 1940, would accompany her aunt Sukh Devi Paliwal and actively participate in picketing of shops selling liquor and foreign cloth, join demonstrations to oppose *purdah* and motivate women to join the freedom movement. She would also contribute to bonfires of foreign cloth and sing stirring nationalist songs while propagating *charkha* and *khadi*, including the following ditty:

> *Khadi ke reshe reshe mein apnepan ka abhiman bhara,*
> *mata ka isme man bhara, anyayee ka apaman bhara.*
> *Khadi ke reshe reshe mein apne bhai ka pyar bhara,*
> *maa bahino ka satkar bhara bachchon ka madhur dular bhara.*[35]

A free translation of the above lines would be

> Every fibre of *khadi* symbolizes the pride of affinity
> The dignity of the mother[land] and humiliation of the oppressor
> Every fibre of *khadi* stands for brotherly love
> The respect of mothers and sisters and the sweet fondness of children.

Another young volunteer in 1940 was 16 year-old Kamla Sharma, daughter of well-known revolutionary Sriram Sharma. She wrote a letter to King George V (of Britain) that he (i.e. the British) should leave India. She used to run errands for those who were underground, carry food, garments, messages and other necessary provisions.[36]

In the course of the individual *satyagraha* campaign of 1940–1941, many women volunteers participated and were sent to jail. Among them were Anandi Devi, Vidyawati Rathor, Sukh Devi Paliwal, Vijaya Kumari, Shakuntala, Gaumati Devi and Aasha. Saraswati Devi, who went to jail for six months, left her young children behind. Chandrawati Vibhav served a prison term of nine months with her three year old son, while Jaya Devi Sharma who remained in prison for a year kept her two month old daughter with her. Many of these volunteers were

Chandrawati Mishra

Jaya Devi Sharma

soon behind bars again after the announcement of the Quit India Movement on 9 August 1942.[37]

The social depth of the movement of 1942 can be seen from the fact that 12 year-old Saroj Rawat was instrumental in stopping the salute to the British flag in her school, Kanya Pathshala, Singigili in July 1942. The salute was part of the Girl Guides Training; she persuaded the students to refuse the salute till the flag was replaced with the Indian tricolour. As this could not be done the Girl Guides training was stopped by the school authorities. On 9 August 1942 the day the Quit India Resolution was to be passed, Saroj and her school mates planned to call a strike in the school. Students of the senior most classes i.e. VII and VIII blocked all the steps leading to the class rooms and did not permit any student to pass through, only teachers were permitted. Due to this the school remained closed. Saroj acknowledged the role and support of the teachers who did not take any action against the students.[38] At the very beginning of the Movement on 12 August 1942 Vidyawati Rathor was arrested and she came out of prison on 2 November 1943. Gaumati Devi was arrested on 16 August 1942 and kept under surveillance till 9 May 1943.[39]

Young educated women and often young girls played a big role in the revolutionary movement of 1942 in Agra. Though all were fervent admirers of Gandhi, his *Do or Die* slogan motivated many to be prepared for all sacrifices. The clandestine transport of weapons and explosives from one state to another was usually the work of women as they were less likely to be suspected.[40]

Bhagwati Devi Paliwal, who had a baby daughter, was the only person in her family who was outside jail in August 1942. She volunteered to carry explosives from Delhi to Agra and was successful on two occasions. The explosives were used to blow up the Income Tax Office in Agra, railway tracks and jail precincts. The third time, her male companion who was a young boy, aroused the suspicions of the police and she was arrested with the explosives. Despite relentless questioning and threats by the police and the magistrate she did not divulge any secrets related to the revolutionary movement but asserted that she would repeat her so called crimes so long as her country was in bondage. The trial of Bhagwati Devi went on for over a year while she was kept in Agra jail and during this time she was subjected to inhuman torture and often kept in chains in solitary confinement, but she still refused to reveal anything or apologize. After a year she was transferred to Lucknow Central Jail and her baby daughter remained with her all the time. In prison in Lucknow, she met Vijaya Lakshmi Pandit and Sucheta Kriplani from whom she learnt English and soon passed the Intermediate Examination. She was released much after many others, in 1946.[41]

Chandrakanta Misra was a young married woman with children and had passed Intermediate and Visharad Examinations; she used to cut railway tracks and electric wires after she joined the revolutionaries with her brother, Kunwar Bahadur Misra. She was arrested and first lodged in Agra district jail but due to her rebellious behaviour she was transferred to Fatehgarh jail. Here she undertook the responsibility of making the women prisoners conscious of their rights as political prisoners. Hence when they were asked to make rope from hemp she burnt it and the fire was used for warmth as the weather was very cold. When the female warden harassed her she vigorously pulled her hair and when the jailer came on his rounds all the co-prisoners made a noise by beating their utensils and none stood up in his honour. This resulted in her being treated as a dangerous criminal; for three months she was kept in solitary confinement. She was then transferred to the jail in Varanasi and was finally released in 1944. In jail she had one of her children with her.[42]

Sukh Devi Paliwal was arrested in September 1942 and went to prison for the eighth time. On 9 October 1942, the day of Deepawali it was the turn of 12-year-old Satyawati Paliwal to offer *satyagraha*. She led a demonstration to Kinari Bazaar and began to deliver a speech. In the meantime the police began a lathi-charge and tried to snatch the national flag from her hand. It was handed to her sister-in-law, Sarla Devi Paliwal, who was also arrested, and the flag was taken by two young male volunteers. They were beaten and all four were sent to jail. The trial of Satyawati went on for three months. She was sentenced on 13 January 1943 to rigorous imprisonment for 18 months. She was released in the middle of 1944.[43]

Poornima Devi, a young married woman of 22, used to transport weapons from one state to another. On the night of 7 December 1942, she was arrested from her house during a secret meeting. The police tried to involve her in a conspiracy case but failed. She was transferred from Agra Jail to Lucknow Central Jail where she met Sucheta Kriplani, Acharya Shanti Devi, Tara Agarwal and Vidyawati Rathor. Although she became seriously ill, she was considered too dangerous to be released on parole. She was finally released in 1945.[44] Premvati Misra was another active member of the revolutionary group in Agra. She specialized in providing clothes for disguise to those who were underground, like costumes of *pandits* and *maulvis*. She was arrested on 9 December 1942 and went to prison with her six year old son. Her daughter was born in prison.[45]

Saroj Rawat, barely 13, and her mother Satyawati Rawat, and Kamla Sharma, led joint demonstrations, holding national flags, on 13 February 1943, and congregated at the crossing of Kinari Bazaar. All three were arrested and awarded prison terms; Satyawati Rawat was sentenced to18 months imprisonment and Kamla and Saroj were each sentenced to one year imprisonment. After a few months, the two girls were shifted to Lucknow Central Jail, while Satyawati was transferred to Benares Jail. When Saroj came out of jail her old school permitted her to resume her studies but when she had to be admitted to a higher class in a new school her prison term became a disqualification.

After great difficulty, Murari Lal Inter College admitted her (in December 1944) but only after her father wrote a stern letter from his prison to the trustees of the college.[46]

Saroj Gaurihar

The turbulent and radical phase of the *Quit India* Movement was over by late 1942, but the popular expression of hostility towards British Rule continued unabated through 1943. There were many women volunteers in Agra who chose to go to prison during 1943 after participating in *satyagraha*. Anandi Devi served a prison term of 18 months, and Parvati Devi was arrested in June 1943 and remained in prison for two-and-a-half years. Sharbati Devi alias Vijaya Kumari was arrested on 10 February 1943 and was imprisoned for a year. Saran Kumari and Akshai Kumari, two young girls, were sentenced on 13 January 1943 to 16 months in prison.[47]

On the basis of responses of the political activists who were interviewed, a short comparative analysis is attempted *vis-à-vis* women's participation in the two major movements of 1930–1932 and 1940–1942 in Agra, though it does reflect to some extent the general picture in the country. As far as the general level of women's participation in the mass phase of the national struggle is concerned, the two activists – Saroj Gaurihar and Bhagwati Devi Paliwal – were unequivocal in their response. Saroj said that the proportion of women's participation in the freedom struggle was in no way lower than that of men, while Bhagwati asserted that it was much more, especially in the Movement of 1942 when women proved themselves to be more adept in the clandestine ways with which the revolution was kept active. Saroj Gaurihar makes a further analysis of the kind of women's involvement in the two major movements.

In the movement of 1930–1932, women, Saroj said, were generally from ordinary domesticated backgrounds. Rural participation was high, and women's mobilization was huge, for example, in picketing shops, schools, offices, making bonfires of foreign cloth, holding demonstrations and shouting national slogans. Moreover these 'ordinary women', when they stepped out of their homes to participate in public activity would usually forget that they were housewives with domestic responsibilities; they became patriots fighting for their country. Their leaders were often mature educated women and their enthusiasm remained unabated all through. After being arrested, especially in 1930, these volunteers were hauled off in police trucks and taken outside city limits where they were off-loaded and left to trudge back home as best as they could. In 1931 and 1932 they were given prison sentences ranging from two to six months. Saroj Gaurihar said it would be impossible to make a list of all those women, as there were too many of them. Bhagwati Devi agrees that the number of women volunteers in the movement of 1930–1932 was much higher.

The national movements of 1940–1941 and 1942–1943 were different from the earlier movement of 1930–1932 in another respect, according to Saroj Gaurihar. The emphasis in the later movements, was on individual resistance; in such cases, the volunteer participated after due deliberation, knowing well that she would be arrested. Most of these volunteers were educated women from middle- and upper-middle-class families, and several of them were veterans of the earlier movement. This also explains the fewer number of women volunteers in these movements. The factor of education, said Saroj Gaurihar, became important as the level and spread of education had increased by 1940. Women volunteers in the movement of 1942–1943 were given prison sentences ranging from a minimum of one to three years, often with solitary confinement or kept in chains as they were considered potentially dangerous.

There were many women in Agra, as in some other places, who did not come out on the streets or go to jail during the national movement but were just as much responsible for sustaining the movement. These women, remaining at home, fully supported their husbands, fathers, brothers, sons and sisters while suffering great deprivation silently. They provided the material support without which no activist could function. Among such women were Krishna Shiromani, Saraswati Devi Paliwal, Vatsala Kunte, Manorama Chauhan, Rameshwari Shiromani, Bhagwati Devi Jain, Mani Behan and countless others.[48]

This account of women freedom fighters of Agra cannot be concluded without a few words on their lives after the country achieved Independence. For most of these volunteers, freedom of the nation was the ultimate goal, and they had no desire for political activism for its own sake. Many of them had suffered a lot because of domestic instability; hence, after Independence, they generally devoted themselves to reorganizing their family lives. Only a few who had political concerns or belonged to families of political leaders entered the political arena. Yet, said Saroj Gaurihar, and this is a fact, the state assembly elections of 1946 and 1951 showed a much higher number of female winners compared to the later elections.

Among those women volunteers who were active in the social or political field in Agra, even after independence, were Vidyawati Rathor, Damayanti Devi Chaturvedi, Premwati Misra, Angoori Devi Jain, Chandrakanta Misra, Champawati Singh, Bhagwati Devi Paliwal, Jaya Devi Sharma, Kamla Sharma and Saroj Gaurihar.[49]

NOTES

1. *CWMG*, Vol. 19, p. 18. Gandhi addressed a separate meeting of students after the public meeting on Non-Cooperation chaired by Abul Kalam Azad at Agra on 23 November 1920. *The Leader* of 26 November 1920 carried a detailed account of Gandhi's speech to the students.

2. *The Leader*, 27 November 1922, p. 7.
3. Ibid., 16 December 1922, p. 9.
4. Ibid., 9 December 1922, p. 6.
5. *Smaranika* (A Compendium on Women Freedom Fighters of Agra). Golden Anniversary Number 1998, Vanita Vikas, Agra.
6. *CWMG*, Vol. 41, pp. 378–379.
7. *Smaranika.*
8. *The Leader*, 25 April 1930 and 26 April 1930.
9. Daughter of Parvati Devi.
10. *Smaranika.*
11. Ibid.
12. This interview was recorded on 27 July 1999 at the residence of Dr Bina Misra (Head, Department of Ophthalmology), in the District Hospital, Agra.
13. *The Leader*, 24 August 1930; *Smaranika*, Agra Ki Mahilayen.
14. *Smaranika*, Smt. Champawati.
15. *Smaranika*, Agra Ki Mahilayen.
16. *The Leader*, Allahabad, Wednesday, 18 July 1930.
17. *The Leader*, Allahabad, Wednesday, 30 July 1930.
18. *Smaranika*, Sukh Devi Paliwal.
19. *Smaranika*, Vidyadhari Jauhari.
20. *The Leader*, Allahabad, 24 August 1930.
21. *Smaranika*, Agra ki Mahilayen.
22. National Archives, New Delhi. Fortnightly Report on the Internal Political Situation in India for the Month of December 1930; File No. 18/XIII/1930– Political, 1930, Govt. of India. Also, *Smaranika*, Agra Ki Mahilayen.
23. *Smaranika*, Angoori Devi Jain, Mata Parvati Devi and Vidyadhari Jauhari.
24. Chintamani Shukla, *Agra Janpad ka Rajnaitik Itihas*, pp. 181–182.
25. *Smaranika*, Agra Ki Mahilayen.

26. National Archives: Fortnightly Report, November 1930, File No. 18/ XII/30 – Political; Fortnightly Report, February 1932, File No. 18/4/32 – Political.
27. *Smaranika*, Agra Ki Mahilayen.
28. Interview with Saroj Gaurihar, daughter of Satyawati Rawat, in August 1999, at F-62, Professor Colony, Kamla Nagar, Agra.
29. *Smaranika*.
30. Interview with Bhagwati Devi Paliwal.
31. P.D. Reeves, B.D. Graham and J.M. Goodman, *Handbook to Elections in Uttar Pradesh: 1920–1951*. New Delhi: Manohar Book Service, 1978, p. 307.
32. UPLAD, Vol. XIV, pp. 490–491.
33. *Police Abstracts of Intelligence*, UP, No. 48/1937, 27 November – 4 December, p. 663.
34. Interview with Saroj Gaurihar. Jagan Prasad Rawat was himself a celebrated Congress activist and lawyer, who held ministerial positions in successive Congress Ministries.
35. *Smaranika*, Satyawati Paliwal.
36. *Smaranika*, Kamla Sharma.
37. *Smaranika*.
38. Interview with Saroj Gaurihar.
39. *Smaranika*.
40. Interviews with Bhagwati Devi Paliwal and Saroj Gaurihar.
41. Interview with Bhagwati Devi Paliwal.
42. *Smaranika*, Smt. Chandra Kanta Misra.
43. *Smaranika*, Satyawati Paliwal.
44. *Smaranika*, Poornima Devi.
45. *Smaranika*, Premwati Misra.
46. Interview with Saroj Gaurihar.
47. *Smaranika*.
48. Ibid.
49. Ibid.

Chapter 6

Women of Almora Arise

Almora district presents an interesting example of women's mobilization during the freedom struggle despite the material conditions of underdevelopment and physical remoteness. The social custom of *purdah* was another negative factor as it led to the automatic segregation of the sexes with women of the upper and middle classes generally being confined within their homes.

However, there were some mitigating factors. One was the pioneering work of the Arya Samaj and some Christian missionaries who spread literacy and social awareness particularly among women during the early decades of the 20th century.[1] Important instruments for spreading political consciousness were the nationalist weekly *Shakti*, published from Almora, and Gandhi's journals, *Young India* and *Navjivan*, which had a wide circulation. Snehlata Joshi, an activist of Nainital, now settled in Haldwani, describes *Shakti* as the *sandesh-vahak* (messenger) of Kumaon.

A very significant event of the freedom struggle in Kumaon was the spontaneous renunciation of the oppressive practice of *coolie begar* in January 1921. Under this practice, British officers posted in or visiting the territory forced the local people to carry all their baggage over the hilly terrain paying only a pittance in as wages. The baggage sometimes included 'forbidden' articles like beef and pet animals.[2] The occasion for the public repudiation of this practice was a festival of great religious significance. Popular leaders, including stalwarts like Badri Dutt Pande, also known as *Kumaon Kesari*, Hargovind Pant and Victor Mohan Joshi, chose the *Uttarayani Mela*[3] and the famous pilgrimage centre of Bageshwar (in Almora district) to proclaim the end of *coolie begar.* At the same time all official records and books relating to the practice were thrown into the confluence (regarded as sacred) of the two rivers, Gomti and Saryu. The crowds that had gathered there took a collective oath that they would never again work as forced labour. This event had a deep social and political impact over the entire region.[4]

The movement for the uplift of Nayak women in the 1920s also created a stir in Kumaon. These women belonged to the backward class and were constrained to engage in prostitution for a living. Govind Ballabh Pant strongly advocated their cause in his speeches in the UP Legislative Council[5] and was eagerly supported by Gandhi when he toured Almora in 1929.[6]

Another factor which roused the patriotism of the people was the tragic death of Lala Lajpat Rai in December 1928. This caused deep anguish to many nationalists.[7] Finally Gandhi's tour of Almora region in 1929 led to a consolidation of national consciousness and laid the ground work for the movements of mass mobilization.[8]

Gandhi toured Kumaon region in June 1929 and as usual struck the most poignant chords of the social situation prevailing there, namely, unemployment, migration, liquor addiction and untouchability. In his speech at Nainital on 14 June 1929 he said that the people had given up their most important occupations, that is, hand-spinning and hand-weaving, adopted foreign cloth and thereby impoverished themselves and this in turn had led to

Mahatma Gandhi in Almora, 1929

migration. He asked all 'brothers and sisters' to give up 'fear and foreign cloth'. Only the *charkha* would satisfy hunger and bring them *swaraj* as it would give 'life to thousands of women'. They should therefore wear only rough hand-made cloth.

Gandhi also asked his audience to give up liquor addiction as it only led to ruin like it had ruined the Yadavas (in the aftermath of the *Mahabharata* conflict). The other conditions of *swaraj* were, he said, communal harmony and eradication of untouchability without which the Hindu religion would be wiped out, for it was based on the principle of *Advaita*, that is the oneness of all living beings.

The urgency of political mobilization was underscored by Gandhi wherever he went as he asked people to become 4 anna members of the Congress. By doing so they would have to pledge themselves to 'achieve *swaraj* through peaceful and honest means'. In a special effort to recruit women in the national cause he asked them to 'volunteer to donate jewellery'.

As in Agra, local representatives presented Gandhi with two beautiful boxes which he appreciated but politely declined saying he had no place to keep them. Always in need of funds for *khadi* work Gandhi told them, 'I would like to strike a bargain with you; you pay me a good sum and buy them!'[9] On 15 June, Gandhi addressed a women's meeting where he urged them to adopt *charkha* and *swadeshi* and thereby make the nation and themselves self-reliant.[10]

On 16 June 1929, Gandhi spoke at Prem Vidyalaya, Tadikhet (Almora District), an institution that had been established in 1921 during the Non-Cooperation movement. The occasion was the celebration of its anniversary. As the trustees gave a litany of their woes to Gandhi his response was simple – 'self-purification' which, he explained, meant 'giving up selfishness and parochialism'. He urged them to enlarge their vision and think not only in terms of their family or village but also their province, their country and finally the world.[11]

An effective and popular means for the transmission of the new ideas and approaches to remote corners of Kumaon and Garhwal regions were the nationalist songs and poems composed in the local idiom by Gauridatt Pande, better known as 'Gaurda'. His themes ranged from forest rights, *charkha* and *swadeshi* to 'economic exploitation, untouchability and other social problems'.[12] One example is quoted here in its Hindi meaning:

Van-vriksha, benap jamin, nadi ghati ki panchakkiyan
sab chhin gaeen
nadiyon mein machhali marane ka bhi hamein adhikar
nahin raha,
jangal ke kanoon se pashudhan ka hras ho gaya
hamein rone bhi to nahin dete, jaban par pratibandh hai
ab dekhte kya ho Kumaun ke vasiyon?
phoota kathauta bhi to nahin bacha.

The following is a free translation of these lines:

> Forests, trees, unmeasured land, rivers, valleys, watermills all
> Have been snatched away
> We do not have the right to catch fish in the rivers
> Our cattle wealth has gone because of forest laws
> They don't even let us cry as there are restrictions on
> our expression
> What are you looking at people of Kumaon?
> Not even a broken penny is left.[13]

Through Gaurda's songs *charkha* and *takli* became part of everyday life in Kumaon.

Kunti Devi Verma

According to Kunti Devi Verma (one of the foremost political activists of Almora and Nainital), women were attending public meetings near the Nanda Devi temple and the Narain Tiwari Deval[aya] in Almora in the course of the Non-Cooperation movement from 1920 to 1922. During festivals like Holi, and at other private and public functions, women would sing national songs instead of the traditional ballads. Plying of *charkha* had become popular among men and women and wearing *khadi* became symbolic of national honour.[14] According to Mrs Hemlata Pande, daughter-in-law of Sri Badri Datt Pande, a towering nationalist acclaimed as *Kumaon Kesari* ('Lion of Kumaon'), Snehlata Joshi and Kunti Devi Verma, it was a common practice for women to give a ceremonial send-off to *satyagrahis* going to jail by anointing them with *tilak* and showering them with flowers.

Vishni Devi Sah was another leading political worker of Kumaon. Like Kunti Devi Verma she was widowed at a very young age and had a small son. She had little education, but this in no way undermined her social and political activities. In 1930 Vishni

Vishni Devi Sah

Durgadevi Pant

Tulsi Rawat

Devi, Durga Devi Pant, Tulsi Devi Rawat, Bhakti Devi Trivedi and Bacchi Devi Pande organized a women's group with over a 100 volunteers.

The launching of the salt *satyagraha* by Gandhi in April 1930 led to the first public demonstrations of women in Almora. On 25 May 1930, Congress leaders there decided to hoist the national flag over the Municipal Building, and with this intention, Victor Mohan Joshi and Shanti Lal Trivedi led a procession of Congress volunteers which included women. They were stopped on the way by armed Gorkha military police who asked them to disperse. On their refusal to do so they were violently attacked, with the result that Victor Mohan Joshi received fatal injuries and Shanti Lal Trivedi several fractures.[15] This tragic incident fuelled the enthusiasm of all nationalists who were now determined to hoist the tricolour flag over the Municipal building.

A delegation of five women, all belonging to Jauhari Mohalla of Almora, namely Kunti Devi Verma, Mangla Devi Verma, Bhagirathi Verma, Jiwanti Devi Thakurani and Revati Devi Verma, decided to go on their own to raise the national flag. They were fully supported by the foremost leaders of the time, including Badri Dutt Pande and Devi Dutt Pant, and were ultimately successful in their purpose.[16]

During 1930 and 1932, we find women activists of Almora district participating and sometimes leading demonstrations and picketing shops selling foreign goods and liquor.[17] Police came down hard on these activities from January 1932 and arrests followed. Vishni Devi was given rigorous imprisonment for two months and a fine of Rs. 10 in default of which her prison term was extended by a month. Jiwanti Devi and Bhagirathi Verma were awarded similar sentences while Harpriya Devi was given a harder sentence of one year. The prospect of jail did not frighten any of them, in fact Vishni Devi used to sing:

Jail na samajho biradar jail jane ke liye
yah Krishna mandir hai, prasad pane ke liye.

A free translation of these lines would be:

Brother, do not think of going to jail as imprisonment
It is the temple of Krishna, to receive his blessing.

Kunti Devi Verma was more enterprising. In 1932 she went to Haldwani with a group of political activists and took up the responsibility of picketing foreign cloth shops there. The group was joined there by Padma Devi Joshi, Bhagirathi Devi and Pani Devi Joshi. All these *satyagrahis* were arrested and sent to prison for varying terms.[18]

Immediately after coming out of prison in May 1932, Vishni Devi took up the work of propagating *khadi* with missionary zeal.

Bhagirathi Devi

Almora had no shops selling *khadi* at that time, while a *charkha* was sold for ten rupees. Vishni Devi not only had the price reduced to five, but also visited individual homes to sell the *charkha* and teach the people to ply it. In the course of this work she persuaded the women to come out of their homes and participate in public activities. She was arrested again on 7 July 1933 and was sent to Fatehgarh jail for a sentence of nine months and a fine of Rs. 200, in default of which her term was extended by a few months.[19]

Indian officers in the British Government may not have had overt sympathy for the national movement, but often their wives were openly supporting it. One such was Ganga Devi Joshi, wife of the Civil Surgeon (also the Jail Superintendent) of Almora in the 1920s and early 1930s. She always wore *khadi,* plied the *charkha,* helped the families of political prisoners and during the Quit India movement, when she was in Nainital, invariably gave shelter to the underground activists, including Shyam Lal Verma and Shanti Lal Trivedi. The police did not suspect her, being the wife of a senior officer in the British Government. Ganga Devi is also remembered for her voluntary support of many young widows and needy children. After India became independent she took charge of the Mahila Ashram in Nainital which had 90 inmates.[20]

Very little is known outside Kumaon about the mass mobilization that occurred in the rural parts of Almora district, particularly in Sult and Salam.[21] The *Second Bardoli* was the name given to the quiet revolution which took place in Sult. Institutions of local self-government and *panchayats*, that is, people's courts, were set up as early as 1921. It was one such court in September 1930 that compelled the Magistrate to award Rs. 5 as compensation to the villagers for the damage done to their crops by the mounted police. A *panchayat* also decided on the social boycott of a White sergeant as the symbol of an oppressive regime. The forest *satyagraha* of 1930 led to brutal repression in which about 100 volunteers were mercilessly beaten and then arrested.

Women were in the forefront of the Individual *Satyagraha* campaign between 1940 and 1941. As propaganda was of the essence, Kunti Devi Verma with a band of women volunteers toured Haldwani, Kaladungi and Kotabagh. In Kota Patkot she was joined by Chandra Devi Verma, Bhavani Devi Joshi, Saraswati Devi and other women who together carried the message of *satyagraha* on foot to Don Parewar, Okhaldunga, Talliseti, Vetalghat, Simlakha and Maghera. Kunti Devi remembers that wherever they went the public responded warmly and many joined them as they moved on. After reaching Nainital they moved about in batches delivering anti-War speeches but were not arrested. Finally, they were all arrested when they encroached on the Secretariat and the Governor's Residence. Some were given light sentences, but Kunti Devi Verma and Chandra Devi Verma of Patkot were given rigorous imprisonment of six months each, together with fines.

Vishni Devi was arrested and imprisoned during the Individual *Satyagraha* campaign. Haruli Devi of Bageshwar, who belonged to a Rajput family, was also imprisoned. She had earlier broken social conventions by stopping Gandhi's *doli* (palanquin) when he was touring the area and declared her intention to do his *aarti*.[22]

Another example of intense rural mobilization in the Salam area may be mentioned here. While Ram Singh Azad, a well-known freedom fighter, was touring villages to enrol volunteers for the Individual *Satyagraha* campaign he stopped at the house of Pratap Singh in Malla Salam. Pratap's mother, Durga Devi, put the hand of her younger son Puran Singh in Azad's hand and said, 'Now I am handing him over to you for serving the nation, you may send him to jail or hang him for the country'. With these words, she anointed her son with *tilak* and sent him off with Ram Singh Azad on 24 March 1941. The same lady donated one of her two gold ear-tops to the *Gandhi Smarak Nidhi* saying she would keep one for the cost of her funeral. Even this piece of jewellery was donated to the National Security Fund when China invaded India.[23]

The Quit India Movement also brought out women activists in Almora District despite the brutal repression let loose by the government. Distributing proscribed literature and helping underground political workers were the usual tasks undertaken by them. Radha Devi, a widow in Gola village in Ranikhet *tehsil*, was sentenced to six months rigorous imprisonment on 8 March 1943. She was sent out of the United Provinces and kept in Hissar jail in Punjab. Later she was transferred to Lahore jail. Malti Devi Bhatt, also of Ranikhet, was given a similar sentence. She was sent to Lahore jail on 8 May 1943.[24]

The Quit India Movement claimed many lives as unarmed crowds challenged the police. Confiscations of property of underground activists and their subsequent auction did not deter the people. There was wholehearted participation by the women in all the activities. Many sold their jewellery, while others cut down their children's food to be able to send food to those who were underground for months at a stretch. There were incidents when women attacked government officials with sickles as they came to threaten or demoralize them and get information about the absconders.[25]

Sarla Behen

The phenomenon of *Stri Shakti*, that is, women's power, in Kumaon, had been specially noted by an English woman settled in India. She was Sarla Behn, the name given by Gandhi; her original name was Catherine Mary Heilman. She became the Mahatma's disciple and was appointed manager of the Chanauda Ashram in Almora. She has written that whether it was the field, home or jungle, women managed everything. During the Quit India campaign, she recounts that all the men working in the Ashram were arrested or absconding. Thereafter, the police auctioned their property and began harassing and threatening the women left behind. Those who tried to help these women were also threatened. In this situation women who had some land managed by tilling it personally or putting it under share cropping, reared cattle, sold milk, spun woollen yarn, knitted sweaters and sold them. In the evenings, the same women would gather together and dance and sing because going to jail for national activities was a matter of honour to them.

Sarla Behn recalls that one of the inmates of the Ashram who was absconding was sentenced to be hanged. A teacher friend gave him shelter but soon the teacher was transferred. Undeterred his wife continued to shelter the fugitive for months and so successfully that the police could not trace him. In another village, after the arrest of a man and auctioning of his land, his wife and children were brought to the verge of starvation. Sarla Behn, before going to jail herself in 1942, managed to leave some food grains with the family and also got some of their mortgaged land released. When Sarla Behn came out of jail sometime later she was surprised to find the family happy and healthy. Upon asking her, the mother replied that the food grains left by Sarla Behn sustained them for some time. Thereafter, her children worked on the field while she collected firewood from the jungle and sold it and did other manual labour. As a result, there was enough to eat and wear, and one son was even going to school. Sarla Behn wrote that it was because of this indomitable spirit in the women of Kumaon that they were later able to carry on the antiliquor agitation.[26]

I would like to conclude with a few words about Vishni Devi Sah, who was perhaps the heroine of the national movement in Almora. In 1934, she was elected to the Executive Committee of the District Congress. Soon after she was awarded a certificate of excellence for the *swadeshi* exhibition put up by her in Bageshwar from 10 to 15 January 1935. Together with Vijaya Lakshmi Pandit, she hoisted the national flag in Nanda Devi grounds and over the new Congress building at Motia Dhara on 23 July 1935. This honour was again bestowed on her on 26 January 1940. She was appointed manager of a new spinning centre opened near Nanda Devi on 17 April 1940. On Independence Day, 15 August 1947, she led the mile-long procession in Almora carrying the national flag.

The *Amrita Bazar Patrika* noted on 30 October 1930 that Almora and Nainital led the Civil Disobedience Movement in the United Provinces and particularly Almora where the role of Vishni Devi was first and foremost. The following lines were popular about her:

Khaddar ki hi dhoti pahane aur khaddar ka hi kurta
ek haath mein khaddar ka jhola aur duje mein surajayee tiranga.

A free translation of these lines would be:

Wearing a *khaddar* sari and a *khaddar* kurta
A *khaddar* bag in one hand and a sunlit
Tri-colour flag in the other!

Unfortunately after independence, Vishni Devi, like several volunteers in the struggle for freedom received no recognition nor were her talents utilized. She lived in penury and died in 1974 at the age of 73.[27]

Perhaps the general remoteness and lack of development in Kumaon region explains this tragedy because this was not a common phenomenon in the other districts studied in the foregoing pages.

NOTES

1. Based on interviews with Pt. Nityanand Misra, historian and retired teacher of Birla Public School, Nainital, and Ms Snehlata

Joshi, activist, retired teacher and daughter of Ganga Devi, freedom fighter of Almora and Nainital, May 1998.

2. *Smarika,* Compendium on Freedom Fighters of Almora District, District Coordination Committee, Almora, 1975, p. 59.
3. The time when the sun moves to the northern hemisphere, marking the beginning of the solar month of *Magh* also known as *Makar Sankranti.*
4. *Smarika,* p. 24. For a historical review of the *coolie begar* issue, see Shekhar Pathak, 'The *begar* Abolition Movements in British Kumaun', *Indian Economic and Social History Review,* Vol. 28, No. 3, pp. 261–279.
5. Interview with Snehlata Joshi.
6. *CWMG,* Vol. XLI, p. 170.
7. Interview with Snehlata Joshi.
8. Sudha Joshi, *Kurmanchal Kesari.* Agra: Chaturvedi Prakashan Samiti, 1970, p. 94.
9. *Aaj* (Hindi), 4 July 1929.
10. Ramnath Suman, *Uttar Pradesh Mein Gandhiji.* Lucknow: Publication Division of the Information Department, UP, 1953.
11. *CWMG,* Vol. 41, pp. 57–58.
12. *Smarika,* pp. 47-49; Binapani Joshi, *Uttarakhand Ki Samajik Hulchalon Mein Mahilaon Ki Bhumika.* Almora: Almora Publications, 1981, p. 295.
13. English translation by author.
14. *Smarika,* p. 99.
15. Ibid., p. 2.
16. S. Joshi, *Uttarakhand Ki Samajik Hulchalon,* p. 295.
17. *Kurmanchal Kesari,* pp. 120–121.
18. *Smarika,* p. 100.
19. S. Joshi, *Uttarakhand Ki Samajik Hulchalon,* pp. 295–296.
20. Interview with Snehlata Joshi.

21. National Archives, New Delhi, *Fortnightly Report on the Internal Political Situation in India*, Home Department, Government of India, for the Month of July 1930
22. *Smarika*, p. 52.
23. Interview with Mohan Lal Sah, Advocate, Almora.
24. *Smarika*, p. 10.
25. Ibid., p. 8.
26. Ibid., p. 60.
27. S. Joshi, *Uttarakhand Ki Samajik Hulchalon*, p. 296.

CHAPTER 7

Nationalism versus Self-Determination: Upsurge in the Assembly

Elections to the Legislative Assembly of the United Provinces, under the Government of India Act, 1935, were held in February 1937. Despite total rejection of the principles underlying the Act, the Indian National Congress contested the elections on a 'socialist' manifesto. The Congress won handsome victories and formed ministries in six provinces: Madras, Bombay, Central Provinces, Orissa, Bihar and the United Provinces. Later, Congress Ministries were also formed in the North-West Frontier Province and Assam. The only exceptions to the electoral success of the Congress were Bengal, Punjab and Sind.[1]

A total of 13 women were elected to the Legislative Assembly in the United Provinces, nine of them on the Congress ticket, one from the Muslim League, two from the landlord-based National Agriculturist Party of Awadh and one as an independent candidate. In the House of 228 members, the women were heavily outnumbered by their 215 male colleagues.[2] Yet the Congress women were often the most vocal, fiercely nationalistic, quite gender-sensitive, and occasionally severely critical of their own ministers! A few instances of their performance in the Legislative Assembly debates and discussions shall suffice to illustrate the breadth of their political and social vision.

The context was the consideration of the Budget, 1937–1938, and the discussion was on the Demands for Grants, Jails and Convict Settlements. The speaker was Mrs Uma Nehru who represented Farrukhabad District North, a 'General Rural' constituency, and had been in prison herself on several occasions. She gave a long speech, declaiming passionately at times, and had obviously given considerable thought to the subject of prison reforms. At the very outset she drew attention to the condition of women prisoners with these words: 'There is no woman in jail who is not ill,' and the only medicine prescribed was 'quinine mixture'. Uma Nehru was of the opinion that more than money, what was required was a change in 'outlook' and 'mentality' which would enable appropriate reforms in prison conditions. She went on to outline various shortcomings and suggested a variety of remedies, which were imaginative and progressive, and appear relevant even today.

The existential environment of prisons was, in her view, depressing, as the buildings, barracks and cells were such as to hardly permit the free circulation of air or light. Prison Hospitals, she said, did not have medicines; there were no 'special beds' for patients, and the watch and ward staff shouted throughout the night giving no rest to the inmates. She was harshly critical of the routine award of inhuman punishments, such as imposition of hard labour and solitary confinement on the smallest pretext, characterizing them as symptoms of a lack of civilization. She also condemned the practice of distinguishing categories of prisoners by dress and colour of caps and called for the abolition of the conventional four categories – A, B, C and D, affirming that the only distinction ought to be between 'political' and 'non-political'.

Her intervention was marked by great attention to detail. She demanded the adequate and individual supply of soap, hair oil and tooth paste to the inmates instead of the extant 'stingy practices' in this regard but did not forget to praise certain changes that had been made with regard to the supply of utensils and bedding, while recommending some additions for better care. A witheringly satirical remark needs to be quoted: 'I am glad that our Minister has permitted the consumption of cigarettes, tobacco and betel leaf because these things are extremely necessary!'

She made several constructive suggestions for the holistic development and rehabilitation of the prison inmates. One was the formation of committees of prisoners to manage various aspects such as food, sanitation and hospital facilities. Another was that lectures and 'magic lantern classes' (slide shows) should be organized for inmates on subjects like health, hygiene and farming, which ought also to be attended by warders and other subordinate staff. Such means could also be used for sensitizing the staff about handling the prisoners. In order to keep inmates connected to the world outside she desired that they be allowed to listen to the radio. Libraries within prisons, which were in a pitiable condition in her view, should be updated and endowed with books on a variety of subjects like jails, the nation and the world outside, which would benefit the inmates.

Referring to productive activities within the jails, of which she had personal knowledge, Uma Nehru emphasized the production of khaddar and its universal use as the most important occupation and duty and stressed the need for rapid promotion of hand-spinning and weaving as occupations. For women, in addition, she desired provisions for training in vocational skills such as knitting, soap making, oil making, nursing, reading and writing. Concluding her speech with a specific address to the ministers, she expressed the hope that all nationalist prisoners would be released immediately together with those convicts whose terms were near completion. 'I am confident that this will be done soon', she added.[3] Indeed, this expectation was realised without much delay.[4]

Not one to shy away from politically contentious issues, Uma Nehru, on another occasion, confidently defended the Congress opposition to the All-India Federation proposed in the Government of India Act, 1935, in the face of stiff criticism in the Assembly. During the debate on the *Resolution Inauguration of the Proposed Federation*, the Congress was charged with deception insofar as it was actually running the government while claiming to reject the constitution under which it was formed! It was also accused of hankering for power and cooperating with the colonial government instead of undertaking civil disobedience against it.

She began her speech by saying that though she was hurt by such arguments, she wanted to tell her 'brothers' (in the Assembly) that the Congress Party was the main political force in the country, second only to the British Government, and no other political organization could compare with it in scope and impact. As far as the question of undermining the Constitution (the Act of 1935) was concerned, there were a thousand ways of doing so apart from undertaking civil disobedience. She asserted that if only the opposition members in the Assembly had knowledge of history of Western countries like Ireland, they would not give such futile arguments.

The Congress, she said, was constantly battling with the British Government even now over the conditions for Ministry formation[5] and would continue to oppose the arbitrary exercise of power, and this was one reason for accepting office. There was no love for the offices as such, nor were they considered big things by the Congress, she declared. Under no circumstances, she asserted, would the Congress accept the scheme of Federation as the masses had no part in it.[6] This was another reason for accepting office, she affirmed, and Congress would oppose the scheme from this platform (the Legislature) with greater strength. The Congress moreover had to stand firm as the reactionaries (the Hindu Sabha, in this case) had to be kept out at any cost, for they were enemies of the country and would sell it for their selfish interests! Supporting the Resolution, she said that, she agreed with the assertion of Acharya Narendra Deva, one of the founding fathers of the Congress Socialist Party and a widely respected member of the Legislative Assembly, that all should come together in the common struggle for freedom; mere talk and carping would get them nowhere.

Continuing her speech, she called on all members to be forward-looking and reminded them that while Western nations were innovating on a daily basis, legislators in India were still debating whether the Maternity Bill would be good or not for the country! Addressing her Muslim 'brothers', she said that calling themselves minorities all the time and seeking protection on that ground was a 'silly thing' to do: 'You are not in a majority certainly but the first thing that Islam teaches every Muslim child is that he or she cannot remain a slave, therefore please think of your religious teachings and immediately join the Congress as it is the only organization that is fighting for freedom from slavery!' Concluding her speech, she reiterated her support for the Resolution and expressed the hope that when the time came for the Federal scheme, her Muslim 'brothers' would support the Congress even if it meant going to jail from that very place.[7]

Satyawati Devi, Congress woman member representing Muzaffarnagar District West (General Rural), gave evidence of her erudition and patriotism in a singular manner while speaking on the subject of education during the Budget Session of 1937–1938. She began her speech by saying that after food, education was the biggest need of humanity and only those countries had prospered which spent the greatest amounts on education. The existing system of education in India established by the colonial power was the antithesis of real education as its goal was not the holistic development of the personality but to consolidate its rule, and not only reconcile the Indian people to it but make them its instruments. Referring to the views of the great revolutionary Lala Hardayal, she said addiction to British education was making us lose our senses (*yeh British Government ki shiksha hamari jati ko sharab pila kar behosh kar rahi hai)*. She also quoted the historian Titus who had written that after the Roman General Julius Agricola conquered Britain, this very same education policy was followed by the new rulers. The result was that the elite of Britain became admirers of the Roman Civilization and accepted its hegemony. Satyawati Devi also recalled the views of Sir Charles Trevelyan, who had endorsed this statement of Titus, and asserted that the same policy was followed by the British in India with the same result. Educated boys and girls not only aped the manners of the British elite, she said, but were 'ashamed' of their parents who may not have been westernized, yet had sacrificed their all to get them educated!

Echoing the words of Gandhi in *Hind Swaraj*, she declared that the education system established by the British in India had enslaved the people, and it was for this reason that in a political movement the educated were the obstacles while the uneducated masses were much less so. The Non-Cooperation Movement, she said, had as its very important goal the boycott of government schools and colleges and the establishment of national educational institutions. These were generally not successful because the British Government had consistently opposed them. In her view, another major problem of the colonial system of education was that it made students fit only for government jobs which were never in adequate number. That is why there were so many suicides she said, as the sons of the rich could not follow their father's occupation and could not even find lowly paid government jobs!

Explaining her approach to dealing with the problem, she said: 'We need neither better buildings nor Professors from outside, [but] a change of our perception and viewpoint (*drishtikon*). With the funds available we may not be able to change the policy and structure of the education system, but at least the libraries in schools and colleges could contain literature that inspired national pride, so that our students, boys and girls, may understand the nation's plight and their national consciousness is aroused. That way the present education system may not cause as much harm.'[8]

Satyawati Devi demonstrated her keen political insight in the debate on another vital issue, namely the *Resolution re the Constituent Assembly* on 1 October 1937. Responding to the statement of a member in the Assembly that only a bloody revolution could lead to a new Constituent Assembly, she said (affirming another statement of Gandhi in *Hind Swaraj*) that this may be true for other countries but could not be true for India because India had not been conquered by the sword. Referring to the view of J.R. Seeley in *The Expansion of England* that England went to India for trade but got instead a huge empire and that too without spending money or shedding blood, she attributed the easy conquest of India to mutual conflicts of Indian states; when one state would fight the conqueror, another would help the latter. There was no feeling of nationality and national pride. But today, she said, the movement led by the Congress had spread to all corners of the country and the nationalist sentiment was very strong, and asserted that if all joined together to make it stronger, complete independence could be attained very soon!

Addressing the issue of communalism very bluntly she said that there was one community that was attacking the roots of the nationalist sentiment. Giving an example she said, a lady member perhaps of the Muslim League (an obvious reference to Begum Habibullah), had stated that 'if a member of the Muslim League separated from it and joined the Congress without laying down conditions such a person would be a traitor to seven crores of Muslims,' but 'I would tell my sister with great respect that such a person would be a traitor only to the Muslim League whereas those who are trying to destroy national unity would be traitors to 35 crores of Hindustanis!' Addressing the Muslim members Satyawati Devi said that no amount of assurances and conditions would satisfy them if they did not have trust in the Congress that it would protect their rights. The British Government had given so many assurances but how many had been fulfilled, she asked, and called upon them to have faith in their own strength.

She also dealt with the sentiment of 'minorityism'. Referring to the 'lament' of a female Muslim member that Muslims being in a minority were weak like a child, she responded 'you', the community, 'are like our mother and I do not agree that you are like a child and Congress being in a majority is like a mother.' In this context, she reminded her that the Muslims were also strong as they were the 'majority' in Sind, Punjab, the North-West Frontier Province and Bengal. If she felt that the Congress would not do justice towards minorities then the Muslims had the same strength and opportunity in those states where Hindus were a minority. Congress had never asked for protection of Hindu interests in those states she explained, then why did the Muslim member raise this issue of protection of Muslims in Hindu-majority provinces. Why are you afraid, she asked, and concluded with the hope that the proposed amendments would be dropped and all 'Hindu and Muslim brothers and sisters' would join as a nation in bonds of affection and endeavour to free the country.[9]

Muslim League members, such as Mr Nafisul Hasan, representing Etawah and Cawnpore (Kanpur) Districts (Mohammedan Rural), had moved an amendment to the *Resolution re Constituent Assembly* demanding 'only that very right of self-determination for the Muslim community which the main resolution demands for the whole people.'[10] He also expressed the feeling that 'the minorities in this country have got some sort of suspicion against the majority community' and if that was allayed the Muslims would not lag behind anybody in the struggle for the freedom of the country.[11]

Speaking after Mr Nafisul Hasan, Smt. Prakashwati Sud (representing Meerut District North, Women General Rural) said that she had stood up to support the main resolution and oppose the amendments. She began by clarifying that the *Resolution re Constituent Assembly* was against the existing Constitution (the Government of India Act, 1935) which had been unanimously opposed by all the political parties. In the last elections, that is in February 1937, the Congress which had opposed the Act tooth and nail received a big mandate from the people which was further evidence of the public opposition to the Act. The countrywide strike on 1 April 1937 also supported this contention. She then addressed the criticism about office acceptance by the Congress under the Act of 1935, stating that this had been done with the best of intentions and contrary to the 'ulterior motives' of the British Government. In this regard, she quoted Mahatma Gandhi's advice to Congressmen to use the Act of 1935 'in a manner not expected by them (the British) and refraining from using it in a way intended by them'.[12]

Continuing, Mrs Prakashvati Sud said that though she opposed the amendments to the *Resolution re Constituent Assembly* she was of the opinion that the Assembly should not be called immediately as it would require a lot of preparation and hard work. She also said that she was aware of the many obstacles in the running of the Constituent Assembly but was confident that they would ultimately be removed and such impediments would also be overcome in the present Assembly. The Muslim League, she said, had demanded that the 'rights' of Muslims be 'safeguarded' and that they should be granted reservation of seats in the future Constituent Assembly. On the other hand, the Congress had made it absolutely clear she said that the Constituent Assembly shall be based on adult suffrage without any distinction on the basis of religion or sex; hence, the demand of the Muslim League was futile. If all participated in every way in the national struggle for independence no force could snatch our rights, she asserted, and advised the minority party neither to consider itself weak, nor have too many expectations from the Congress; on the contrary, it must make itself so strong that no one could deny its rights or suppress it. 'I shall therefore', she concluded, 'request the Speaker, with his permission, that the amendments be withdrawn'.[13]

Mrs Suniti (spelt as Shuniti at several places in the Legislative Assembly Proceedings) Devi Mitra, representing Rae Bareli District North East (General Rural), gave a powerful speech illustrating the pros and cons of the *Resolution re Constituent Assembly* that was being debated in the Legislative Assembly. It seemed, she said, that those arguing against the Resolution had not read it properly. The first statement of the Resolution, she said, was noncontroversial; the confusion began with the second statement which stated, she quoted, '... for a free India framed by a Constituent Assembly elected on the basis of adult franchise'; the key words were 'free India', she said. This meant that the Constituent Assembly would be formed when India was free; hence, all the amendments become invalid. To quote her: 'When India was ready to be free, nobody would listen to slaves like you and me, and talk of these amendments, conditions, safeguards, would become futile.'

Suniti Devi rhetorically asked as to why everyone had opposed the Government of India Act 1935. The reason, she answered, was that after promising Dominion Status for India, the British Government, when the time came, placed so many safeguards and conditions that the Act became meaningless. Addressing the members of the opposition she said: 'By placing safeguards on the Constituent Assembly of a free India you want to make it meaningless.' She stated that the opposition was under the wrong impression and by their insistence the Constituent Assembly could become a laughing matter!

Another statement in the Resolution which she believed had caused misunderstanding was '...which allows the Indian people full scope for development according to their needs and desires'. This means, she said, that once a country attains freedom and it sits down to plan its Constitution then decisions are taken according to the conditions prevailing then, and the intentions and desires of the representatives of the nation. 'At that time you or I or this House will have no power to dictate terms', and therefore 'the amendments are meaningless and have no relation to the actual Resolution,' she asserted.

Suniti Devi wanted to make another point clear; as so many things had been said in the debate regarding the Resolution, addressing the members who claimed to represent the Muslim community, she said that they were making demands which may cater to the urban areas, whereas 90 per cent of the people in the country lived in the villages. 'If you will go to be villages', she asserted, 'observe their lives, you will understand that they are neither Hindu nor Muslim, nor members of this Assembly, they are only of one kind. They are poor and hungry Hindustani peasants (*kashtkar*). Also the issue of Hindu and Urdu is nonexistent for them, as they speak with one voice, that is, of suffering and grief. They do not care for reservations or separate electorates. The only question before them is of their hunger and security; anyone who will take care of that is their representative.'

Speaking from personal experience she said that she represented a rural constituency and she had ample opportunities for meeting people there. Thousands of poor Hindustanis came to her with their grievances, and they did not think of themselves as Hindu or Muslim and neither did she think of them in this manner. Addressing the Muslim members again through the President, she asked them that when they went to the villages in their constituencies did they listen only to the Muslim grievances and turn out the Hindus. Had they come to the House with this attitude? Was this their understanding of public service? But then they claimed to represent both Hindus and Muslims, 'If you actually understand the meaning of public representation (*numaindigi*), you would not be making these demands', she said.

She concluded by saying: 'I would like to remind you that this is a battle for freedom and free "Bharat" has only one voice. We have to think of how to solve our national problems, particularly of hunger of the people. This cannot be solved without freedom and the nation is all ready for this struggle. No obstacles can stand in its way; they will be swept away and together with them those who plant obstacles.'[14]

From a feminist point of view there was an interesting debate in the Assembly when the discussion on *Rules re the Appointment of Honorary Magistrates* was held on 1 February 1938.[15] There had been no move to appoint women as honorary magistrates till one male member, Kunwar Sir Maharaj Singh, C.I.E. (Indian Christian) moved an amendment in favour of women being appointed to such posts. Smt. Satyavati Devi, the first woman member to speak on the issue, fully endorsed the motion saying that though she had wanted to make the demand herself she did not do so as it may have appeared 'biased' (she used the word 'communal'). Kunwar Maharaj Singh, she said, had through his suggestion given women's rights their proper place and she was grateful to him for that.

Women till sometime ago, said Satywati Devi, had an orthodox view about their position in society. Their role, they believed, was limited to the domestic sphere. This had changed and now they had stepped out of their homes and were excelling in whatever field they chose to go, including the political sphere. Their participation in the struggle for freedom included suffering in prison without demur, heading the All India Congress Committee and successfully taking up and fulfilling all other responsibilities entrusted to them. Under these circumstances she failed to understand, she said, 'why in the sphere of "domestic justice" they could not be trusted', implying that in women's cases, women ought to be the magistrates. 'I feel,' she said, 'women will understand women's problems much better than men.' Her next statement might appear sexist, but she only voiced her 'class' apprehension when she said that it was not appropriate for women to appear before male magistrates. In this context, she cited the standing order of the District Magistrate of Meerut that a special magistrate holding court alone must not hear women's cases. She also felt it essential that women's cases must be heard by women magistrates. With these words she said that she supported Kunwar Maharaj Singh's amendment.[16]

The next female member to speak on the subject was Mrs Suniti Devi Mitra, who gave a fiery speech. She stoutly opposed the previous motion by Kailash Nath Katju, the Minister of Justice, who had said that a twenty-five year old woman had less wisdom and less knowledge than a twenty-five year old man. According to her, this statement was contrary to facts as a man could hardly became serious till the age of 40 while a woman not only became serious but gained a lot of experience by that age which she could put to good use! She was of the opinion that 22 years and 25 years should be prescribed as the ages of appointment, for females and males respectively. Even the clause recommending differential ages of retirement, 55 years and 50 years respectively, for men and women should be reversed, she said, and elaborated: 'I can say with authority that a woman stays stronger than man and she can retain her strength better. But a man often becomes old by the age of 50 begins to stoop and becomes mentally weak. So if 22 years and 55 years which have been recommended for men are recommended for women then it will be a good thing.' On a conciliatory note, she said women do not desire any special concessions; she believed that in the world they had equal roles to play. 'In Hindustan', she said, 'women do not want "favouritism" of any kind. They only want equal rights; if the age recommended for males is 50 then it should be the same for women.'[17]

Joining in the debate on *Rules re the Appointment of Honorary Magistrates*, particularly the issue of age, *vis-à-vis* men and women candidates, Mrs Uma Nehru voiced a feminist perspective. In her speech she first appreciated those male numbers of the House who supported the views of Mrs Suniti Devi Mitra, who had spoken earlier. She observed that there was no particular difference between boys and girls but generally she had noticed that girls were wiser than boys. She said she was opposed to the statement of her 'brother', Mr Krishna Nath Kaul (representing Faizabad District East, General, Rural), who had said that when women became magistrates there would be trouble in the house. It was meaningless to say this, she said, because nowadays women were accomplishing their tasks outside the home with great panache (*khoobi ke saath*). To quote her, 'I would like to reassure my "brother" that in such a situation the woman will keep her home safe from every trouble; in fact it is our men who create the trouble!'

Continuing her intervention in the debate, she said that as far as domestic quarrels were concerned they need not worry. Reassuring the male members she asserted that together with their outside and domestic tasks women could solve the issue of men for 'after all, men are part of the domestic issue!' She said the argument about the question of age, whether 25 or 50 years for men or women, was pointless and the Minister of Justice, she believed, fully understood that. She also suggested that Mr Kaul should withdraw his proposal after hearing the discussions; otherwise a needless controversy would be created. Her final argument was that when women were becoming doctors, professors, lawyers, doubting their ability to become magistrates was hardly right. In fact, she declared, 'why only honorary magistrates, they should be judges also!' Upon the interjection of Pandit Mahabir Tyagi, representing Dehradun District (Urban), that this argument was 'contrary', Mrs Nehru replied: 'Yes, today, everything is contrary. Till women become judges, magistrates, in fact work in every department in Hindustan, the country shall not progress.' Concluding her speech, she hoped 'Kaul Sahab' would withdraw his proposal, otherwise quarrels inside and outside the home would be common.[18]

This account of the participation of women members, particularly of the Congress (who were nine out of the total female membership of thirteen), in the proceedings of the Legislative Assembly (1937–1939) would not be complete without a mention of the deft handling of issues and cut motions by the Minister of Local Self-Government and Public Health, Mrs Vijaya Lakshmi Pandit (who represented Cawnpore District North-East – Women General Rural). A few instances may be cited. The occasion was the discussion on the Budget of 1937–1938, Demands for Grants, Grant No. 16–39, Public Health. In the context of complaints about school health officers, a cut motion had been moved by a member suggesting that the school health officers should be dismissed. She responded by explaining that as their service was essential, instead of dismissing them they should be made to 'work in the correct way'. She assured the House 'that so long as I am here the health officers will have to work at least half as hard as I am prepared to work and the system will change considerably'. She also spoke of concrete measures saying that the whole thing was under consideration and the government intended to make changes by cutting down salaries, putting better and more efficient men in the right place. She therefore requested the 'honourable mover of the motion not to press it, because I really think that bad as they are, they are doing some good'.[19]

The forthright approach of Mrs Pandit and the intentions of the new government, which promised a people's government, were made clear in her speech on the same day as the above instance. She said that so far as the present government was concerned it treated with great respect every cut motion or other suggestion made by the opposite side of the house. She would be particularly grateful, she said, to any member of the House who would consider it worth his while to give her suggestions on the running of her department. To quote her, 'The Congress does not like to talk too much. We shall be judged by our actions and I would request the honourable members to give us a little time to act.'[20]

One of the innovations by her Department of Public Health was the 'imparting of health education in urban and rural areas on an entirely different basis so as to make it more intelligible to the masses, inspire confidence in the public mind and create a desire for the simple rules of health which are so urgently required in this country'. She also outlined the plans of the Government of India and the Provincial Government to deal with the grave problem of malaria and shortage of drinking water in rural areas.[21]

Another instance of her deft handling of policy issues may be observed during the discussion on *The United Provinces Indian Medicine Bill* on 5 July 1939. Chaudhari Akhtar Hussain, a Congress member, had expressed apprehensions over the observations made by the government regarding control of the 'mushroom growth' of institutions of traditional medicine and had moved an amendment to the proposed Bill. Mrs Pandit, as Minister of Local Self-Government and Public Health, explained the position of the government in a such a manner that Mr Husain was led to say 'very lucid speech, if I may say so with respect, of the Hon'ble Minister of Local Self-Government, who has dispelled all those doubts and there is no doubt left in my mind now. I am entirely satisfied with the policy that is now being adopted by the Government, and in view of the assurance given by the Government, there is no necessity now for me to press my own amendment.'[22]

Smt. Vidyawati Rathor, another Congress woman, representing Etah District South (General Rural), asked starred questions on an important administrative matter. The subject was a Government Order (GO) No. 1877-B/1B-145, dated 29 July 1932: 'Combinations of the Posts of Sarishtedar and Stenographer in Less Important Districts'. She asked (Q. No. 61) whether it was a fact that the GO was implemented by the Government as a measure of economy, whenever circumstances permitted. She next asked (Q. No. 62) whether the Government was aware that in paragraph 39 of the Darwin Committee Report it had been pointed out that in commensuration with their pay stenographers in many districts had not enough work and had suggested the combination of the duties of reader and stenographer in the less important districts. Her next question (No. 63) related to asking the government to lay on the table a statement showing the districts and divisional offices in which the Government Order or the recommendation of the Darwin Committee Report had been acted upon as a measure of economy. Her final question (No. 64) on the matter was to ask the Government whether it was aware that in the Settlement Department there existed the system of a combined post of reader and stenographer. In reply Mr Rafi Ahmad Kidwai, the Minister of Revenue, said that the information was being collected and a reply would be given at a later date.[23] Mrs Vidyawati Rathore also spoke on matters relating to provincial excise and prohibition.[24]

Another woman Congress member who participated in the debates asking for better financial allocation for children's health and hygiene and other medical matters was Dr Bolar Thungamma, FRCSE (Benares City Women, General, Urban).[25] Sharmada Tyagi, representing the Congress from Dehradun District (General, Rural) was one of the first to speak on a cut motion moved by an opposition member, criticizing the Congress government's alleged partiality to the tenants. She justified the policy saying the Congress was trying to correct the existing imbalance in the farming sector and strengthen the hands of the tenants.[26]

The foregoing account of the active participation of women members of the Legislative of Assembly, particularly of the Congress in the parliamentary debates, between 1937 and 1939 in the United Provinces, leaves no doubt about their abilities to handle all kinds of issues even difficult and sensitive political ones. Some of these members came from political families,[27] but their views and their functioning left those political strings far behind. The fact that they were educated is indeed basic to positive political orientation, but their perceptions about the contemporary situation and the political, social and economic problems were acquired through personal observations and experiences and hard work in their respective constituencies.

Speeches delivered by the women members of the UP Legislative Assembly in the ongoing debates and discussed in this account surely set aside two fallacies stated in one of the few publications on the record of women legislators in UP – that these members hesitated to express their views on the 'communal question' and that it 'is noteworthy that they speak less than do men in the parliamentary debates'.[28] Considering the fact that there were only 13 women against a mammoth majority of 215 men the performance of these women was truly heroic!

NOTES

1. Bipan Chandra, *India's Struggle for Independence*. New Delhi: Penguin Books, 1989, pp. 322–323.
2. Alphabetical list of members with their constituencies, *Proceedings of the Legislative Assembly of the United Provinces 1937–1939* (in 21 volumes; hereafter *UPLAP*), Vol. 1 (29 July–9 September 1937), pp. vi–viii; Visalakshi Menon, *Indian Women and Nationalism: The U.P. Story*. New Delhi: Shakti Books, Har-Anand Publications, 2003, p. 123.
3. *UPLAP* Vol. 2 (10 September–5 October 1937), 11 September, pp. 93–97.
4. Bipan Chandra, *India's Struggle*, p. 326.
5. The Governor's discretionary powers were questioned by the Congress.
6. The Princely States were to be represented by their rulers.
7. *UPLAP* Vol. 3 (17 January–7 February 1938), 20 January, pp. 501–503.
8. *UPLAP* Vol. 2 (10 September–5 October 1937), Budget 1937–1938, Discussion of Demands for Grant No. 14 – Head of Account: 37 Education, 22 September, pp. 907–908.
9. Ibid., October 1, *Resolution Re Constituent Assembly*, pp. 1577–1578.
10. Ibid., p. 1558.
11. Ibid.
12. B. Chandra, *India's Struggle*, p. 324
13. *UPLAP* Vol. 2 (10 September–5 October 1937), 1 October, pp. 1558–1560.

14. Ibid., pp. 1646–1648.
15. See note 26, Chapter 4.
16. *UPLAP* Vol. 3 (17 January–7 February 1938), 1 February, pp. 1297–1298.
17. Ibid., p. 1304.
18. Ibid., pp. 1305–1306.
19. *UPLAP* Vol. 2 (10 September–5 October 1937), 10 September, p. 28.
20. Ibid., p. 29.
21. Ibid., p. 33.
22. *UPLAP* Vol. 5 (18 May–8 July 1939), No. 11 (days), 5 July, p. 593.
23. *UPLAP* Vol. 11 (21 December 1938 to 13 January 1939), Questions and Answers, 3 January, pp. 110–111.
24. *UPLAP* Vol. 14, pp. 488–491.
25. *UPLAP* Vol. 2 (10 September–5 October 1937), 10 September, pp. 27–28, and Vol. 4 (1–23 March 1938), p. 896.
26. *UPLAP* Vol. 2 (10 September–5 October 1937), 15 September, p. 376; Visalakshi Menon, op. cit., p. 124.
27. Visalakshi Menon, *Indian Women and Nationalism*, p. 126.
28. Ibid, p. 125; S.M. Sayeed, 'Women's Participation in U.P. Politics – A Study of Political Attitudes and Performance of the Women Members of the U.P. Assembly', *Indian Journal of Political Studies*, Vol. 32, 1971, pp. 223–224.

Conclusions

The United Provinces do indeed present an instructive picture of the close relationship between education and political mobilization of women, particularly in the period 1916 to 1942, although the role of Mahatma Gandhi in motivating women and that of institutions like the Arya Samaj and family influences cannot be discounted. The overall position of women's education in United Provinces was of course depressing, but as has been shown in the previous chapters both education and political mobilization of women were largely urban phenomena and reinforced each other. Wherever mobilization of women occurred on a large scale in rural areas it was mainly on account of the efforts of urban women going there and persuading the women there to join them in the national interest.

Official records also point to the fact that political conditions were influencing the spread and level of female education. The *Quinquennial Report on Public Instruction in the United Provinces* of 1922 notes about the progress of female education: 'it is possible that the ferment of politics has created a desire for more knowledge among women.'[1] Total enrolment of Indian girls increased by 21 per cent in the quinquennium, and the growth of collegiate education was its most 'marked feature'. District Board schools, which were mainly primary schools for girls in rural areas, recorded an increase of 55 per cent in the number of scholars. Even the *Quinquennial Report* of 1927[2] shows that Anglo-Vernacular high and middle schools recorded an increase of 73 per cent in enrolment, and this was mainly from among Indian Christians and Hindu girls. The number of vernacular middle schools increased by almost 50 per cent, and the District Board schools showed considerable increase as well.

The year 1930 was the watershed moment in women's political mobilization in the United Provinces. Their prominence in meetings, demonstrations, processions and picketing is repeatedly noted in the Fortnightly Reports on the internal political situation in India, maintained by the Government of India. The report for the second half of May 1930 notes, as a 'disquieting feature', 'the increasing part taken by women in intensifying racial bitterness'[3] and the report for the second half of August 1930 states: 'The great interest taken in the movement by women of all classes is a factor with which we have also to reckon; it apparently extends far beyond the circle of those who make themselves prominent by joining in processions or making speeches.'[4] The role of women in the open defiance of laws is acknowledged again in the report for the second half of October 1930.[5] In these reports the dominance of the Indian National Congress in most districts of the United Provinces, specifically on the local bodies and through them on educational institutions maintained by these bodies, is anxiously noted. The spread of the national movement into the rural areas is also noted.

The *Quinquennial Report* of 1932, in its chapter on female education, records unprecedented progress and clearly relates it to the ongoing political situation. To quote, 'the encouraging feature of the quinquennium is that public opinion in regard to girls' education has changed and in many places and among many communities indifference has been succeeded by appreciation.'[6] As stated in Chapter 1, the Report of the Hartog Committee (1929) affirmed that education was being recognized as a 'matter of primary national importance', essential to 'the difficult task of nation-building.'[7]

The considerable progress at the secondary and middle stage of girls' education continued apace in the quinquennium

1932–1937. The percentage increase of girl students in various stages of instruction during the period was as follows:[8]

Level	*1932*	*1937*	*Increase in percentage*
Colleges	172	379	120
High school	335	823	146
Middle section	4,474	9,154	104
Upper primary	9,390	18,117	71
Lower primary	25,768	34,697	34
Preparatory	61,220	73,612	20

Even the *Quinquennial Report* of 1942[9] notes the expansion of university and college education, though progress at other levels of education was checked due to the economic situation created by the war, which also affected the urban middle class. However, university and college education expanded on account of several factors, such as the general awakening due to the War and the national movement, the expansion of secondary education in the previous quinquennium and the desire for higher education that was quickly spreading among women and the backward classes.[10]

Apart from the women's hostels attached to the Universities of Lucknow, Benares, Allahabad, Agra and Aligarh, another women's college named Mahila Vidyalaya was affiliated to the Lucknow University. The number of women's intermediate colleges rose to 11 with a total enrolment of 4,461.[11] Women's participation in the movements of 1940–1941 and 1942–1943 was not only high but also of a quality different to that of 1930–1932. Women who participated in the individual *satyagraha* campaign of 1940–1941 and also in the Quit India Movement of 1942–1943 did so in their individual capacity and not as a group activity. They undertook Civil Disobedience or engaged in 'terrorist' activity after a great deal of thought, knowing well that they would not only be arrested but may be subjected to inhuman torture in jail. Most of the women in these movements were young and educated, some in colleges and universities, whereas many of the women in the earlier movements were less educated or educated up to the primary level. The patriotism or commitment to the national cause in the women who were active in the earlier movements was not less in any way than those who partook in the later movements, and only the techniques or methods of struggle were different between these two phases in freedom struggle. The factor of women's education became important by the 1930s, as the level and spread of female education had considerably increased by that time, at least in urban areas.

In the Movement of 1930, the British administration had decided not to come down heavily on the women volunteers out of fear of a backlash. Hundreds of women participated in meetings, demonstrations and picketing of shops selling foreign cloth or liquor or government schools and colleges or other government establishments. These women were generally arrested and put into police vehicles and left outside city limits to trudge back home. In 1932 women volunteers who were arrested for Civil Disobedience were generally given simple imprisonment ranging from six months to one year. Similarly, in 1940–1941 the administrative authorities would often not arrest the women who offered individual *satyagraha* though these women continued to do so till they were arrested. Sentences were light, from one month to three months. However, the women who actively participated in the Quit India Movement of 1942 were ruthlessly dealt with. Even girls aged 12 and 13 years were given rigorous imprisonment of 18 months, and in the case of older women it was up to 3 years. Yet there was no dearth of volunteers!

As in the field, the role of the women legislators inside the assembly was quite remarkable. They dealt with a wide range of subjects such as prison conditions, tenancy reforms, cuts in the budget, health and medical concerns, educational restructuring, sensitive political questions like the status of minorities and the future constituent assembly, the federal scheme, the communal question, and administrative issues such as those relating to eligibility for posts and economy in administration.

It may be said, in conclusion, that evidence shows that education, whether of a primary or higher standard, was an important factor in the political mobilization of women in the United Provinces between 1916 and 1942 and of course afterwards. The other important factor, as has been demonstrated, was no doubt the impact of Mahatma Gandhi. In this context, it may be relevant to state that a common feminist argument has been to question the influence of Gandhi on the position of Indian women at a personal and political level. It implies that no real change took place in the lives of the women who participated in the struggle for freedom.[12]

The author seeks to disagree with this view, and it would be appropriate to quote Visalakshi Menon in this regard:

> Of course women had to return to their roles as wives and mothers. But they returned as different women. They had learnt to stand up against injustice. Within the family they were accorded more respect and their sacrifices were recalled with pride. The women who had been involved in the national movement often continued in their own different ways to involve themselves in some public activity.[13]

Another valid counter-argument to the feminist contention was provided by Sucheta Kripalani, a well-known freedom fighter and Chief Minister of Uttar Pradesh from 1963 to 1967. She has been described as 'the best Chief Minister U.P. has had'.[14] To quote her:

> We have not only inspired our men but have stood shoulder to shoulder with them in the ranks of *satyagrahis*. Expectant mothers, mothers with babies in their arms have marched to jail.... And yet they never faltered, never wavered..... They did not flinch before the police batons or the *lathi* charge.... What has been the result? Their emancipation has been automatically accomplished.... We did our duty well and the reward has followed. It has not only given us our rights but our self-respect. We have discovered ourselves to ourselves.[15]

NOTES

1. *Quinquennial Report on Public Instruction in the United Provinces of Agra and Oudh*, 1922, Chapter 7, UP State Archives, Lucknow (hereinafter referred to as QRPI).
2. *QRPI*, 1927.
3. National Archives (NA), *Fortnightly Reports* (FR) on the Internal Political Situation in India, Government of India, Home Department, Secret File No. 18/V/30 Political.
4. NA *FR* File No. 18/IX/30 Political.
5. Ibid.
6. *QRPI*, 1927
7. See note 24 to Chapter 1.
8. *QRPI*, 1927.
9. *QRPI*, 1942.
10. S. Nurullah and J.P. Naik, *A Students History of Education*, p. 322.
11. Ibid.
12. For example, Sujata Patel's 'back-handed swipes' on Gandhi in 'Construction and Reconstruction of Woman in Gandhi', *Economic and Political Weekly*, 23(8), 1988 (327–387), pp. 327, 386. Patel starts out by stating that Gandhi envisaged a significant role for women in Indian society but ends up declaring, 'Gandhi used essentialist arguments to reaffirm the woman's place as mother and wife in the household. He denied her sexual needs, yet emphasized her distinct social role in the family by glorifying some of her "feminine" qualities.'
13. V. Menon, *Indian Women and Nationalism*, p. 171. See also note 1 of the Introduction for the view of Suruchi Thapar-Bjorkert in this regard.
14. These were the words of K.K. Dass, ICS, who served under her, in Verinder Grover and Ranjana Arora, *Great Women of Modern India – Sucheta Kriplani: Her Contribution to Political, Economic and*

Social Development. New Delhi: Deep and Deep Publications, 1993, pp. 314-316.

15. Sucheta Devi [Kriplani], 'Woman and Satyagraha' (5 June 1940), reproduced in *Appendix C* to Visalakshi Menon, *Indian Women and Nationalism*, pp. 181–183.

Bibliography

PRIMARY SOURCES

Annual and Quinquennial Reviews of the Progress of Education in India. New Delhi: National Archives.

Annual and Quinquennial Reports on Public Instruction in the United Provinces. Lucknow: U.P. State Archives.

Census of India, 1881 to 1951.

Collected Works of Mahatma Gandhi [CWMG]. New Delhi: Publications Division, Ministry of Information and Broadcasting, Government of India, and Ahmedabad: Navajivan Trust, 100 Volumes, 1958–1998.

Criminal Record Room Files 1930–32. Criminal Records of Allahabad Collectorate, Allahabad: U.P. Regional Archives.

District Gazetteers of the United Provinces [United Provinces District Gazetteers]. Allahabad: Superintendent, Government Press, 1903–1921.

District Gazetteers of Uttar Pradesh [Uttar Pradesh District Gazetteers]. Lucknow: Government of Uttar Pradesh, 1964 onwards.

Famine Inquiry Commission. Final Report. Delhi: Manager of Publications, 1945.

Finalised Transcripts, Oral History Archives. New Delhi: Nehru Memorial Nehru Memorial Museum and Library, 1966–.

Hajra Begum, ACC No. 613.

Prabhavati Narayan, ACC No. 260.

Fortnightly Reports on the Internal Political Situation in India, 1930–32. Government of India, Home Department, Political. New Delhi: National Archives.

Indian Educational Policy: Resolution of the *Government of India in the Home Department, 11th March, 1904.* Calcutta: Superintendent of Government Printing, 1904.

Indian Education Policy: Being a Resolution issued by the Governor-General in Council on the 21st February 1913. Calcutta: Superintendent of Government Printing, 1913.

Interim Report of the Indian Statutory [Simon] Commission: Review of the Growth of Education in British India [by the Auxiliary Committee of Sir Philip Hartog]. London: H.M.S.O., 1929.

Jayaprakash Narayan Papers (on microfilm). New Delhi: Nehru Memorial Museum and Library (Individual Collections Sl No. 395).

Police Abstracts of Intelligence, U.P. Lucknow: C.I.D. Office.

Proceedings of the Legislative Council, United Provinces, Lucknow: U.P. State Archives.

Proceedings of the Legislative Assembly of the United Provinces. Allahabad: Superintendent, Printing and Stationery, United Provinces. The following volumes were accessed at the Central Library, Banaras Hindu University, Varanasi:

Vol. I: 29 July to 9 September 1937.

Vol. II: 10 September to 5 October 1937.

Vol. III: 17 January to 7 February 1938.

Vol. V: 18 May to 8 July 1938.

Vol. XI: 21 December 1938 to 13 January 1939.

Vol. XIV: [Date not given].

Rameshwari Nehru Papers. New Delhi: Nehru Memorial Museum and Library.

Report of the Committee on Primary Education [Piggot Committee]. Allahabad: Superintendent, Printing and Stationery, United Provinces, 1913–14.

Report of the Conference of Directors of Public Instruction (January 1917). Delhi: Superintendent of Government Printing, 1917.

Report on Primary Education for Boys and Girls in the United Provinces of Agra and Oudh, with Special Reference to Uneconomical & Superfluous Schools by R.S. Weir, Assistant Director of Public Instruction, United Provinces. Allahabad: Superintendent, Printing and Stationery, United Provinces, 1938.

Report of the Primary and Secondary Education Reorganization Committee [Acharya Narendra Deva Committee]. Allahabad: Superintendent, Printing and Stationery, United Provinces, 1939.

Report of the National Committee on Women's Education [Durgabai Deshmukh Committee], *May 1958 to January 1959.* Delhi: Manager of Publications, Government of India, 1959.

Selections from Educational Records Volumes 1 and 2. Calcutta: Superintendent of Government Printing, 1920–22.

Selections from the Records of the Government of India, Department of Education. Calcutta: Superintendent of Government Printing, 1911.

Speeches and Writings of Annie Besant. Madras: G.A. Natesan, 1921.

Speeches and Writings of Sarojini Naidu. Madras: G.A. Natesan, 1920.

Towards Equality: Report of the Committee on the Status of Women in India. New Delhi: Government of India, Department of Social Welfare, Ministry of Education and Social Welfare, 1974.

SECONDARY SOURCES

Ahmad, Imtiaz (ed.), *Modernization and Social Change among Muslims in India.* Delhi; Manohar, 1983.

Ahmad, Karuna, 'The *social context of women's education* in India, *1921–81*: Tentative formulations'. *New Frontiers in Education* 15(3), 1985, pp 1–36.

Amrit Rai, *Premchand*: *A Life*, trans. Harish Trivedi. New Delhi: Oxford University Press, 1982.

Ashraf, U.S. and T.S. Papola, *Problems of Non-Enrolment, Nonattendance and Dropouts in Schools: A Study in Uttar Pradesh*. Lucknow: Giri Institute of Development Studies, 1982.

Baig, Tara Ali (ed.), *Women of India*. New Delhi: Publications Division, Government of India, 1958.

Basu, Aparna, *The Growth of Education and Political Development in India, 1898–1920*. Delhi: Oxford University Press, 1974.

Bhargava, Moti Lal, *History of Secondary Education in Uttar Pradesh*. Lucknow: Superintendent, Printing and Stationery, U.P., 1958.

Bhartiya, Tabassum Nizami, *Lucknow Janpad Ka Rashtriya Itihas*. Lucknow: Uttar Pradesh Sahitya Sadan, 1961.

Bhattacharya, Sabyasachi (ed.), *The Contested Terrain: Perspectives on Education in India*. Hyderabad: Orient Longman, 1998.

Bhatty, Zarina, 'Socialization of Female Muslim Child in U.P.', in Karuna Chanana (ed.), *Socialization, Education and Women*. Delhi: Orient Longman, 1988, pp. 231–239.

Bipan Chandra, Mridula Mukherjee, Aditya Mukherjee, K.N. Panikkar, Sucheta Mahajan, *India's Struggle for Independence*, New Delhi: Penguin Books, 1989.

Brijbhushan, Jamila, Muslim Women in Purdah and Out of it. New Delhi: Vikas, 1980.

Chattopadhyay, Kamaladevi, *Indian Women's Battle for Freedom*. New Delhi: Abhinav Publications, 1983.

Chaturvedi, Sri Narayan, *The History of Rural Education in the United Provinces of Agra and Oudh, 1840–1926*. Allahabad: Indian Press, 1930.

Desai, Neera, *Women in Modern India* (Second edition). Bombay: Vora and Company, 1977.

Desai, Neera, and Maithreyi Krishnaraj (ed.), *Women and Society in India*. Delhi: Ajanta Publications, 1987.

Forbes, Geraldine, *Women in Modern India* (*Vol.IV.2: The New Cambridge History of India*). Cambridge University Press, 1999, pp. 139–154

Gallagher, John, Gordon Johnson, and Anil Seal (ed.), *Locality, Province and Nation*. Cambridge, Cambridge University Press, 1973.

Gandhi, Mohandas Karamchand, *Educational Reconstruction*. Segaon, Wardha: Hindustani Talimi Sangh, 1939.

Gandhi, Mohandas Karamchand, *Hind Swaraj or Indian Home Rule* (1909), edited by Anthony J. Parel. Cambridge: Cambridge University Press, 1997, p. 37.

Gandhi, Mohandas Karamchand, 'Neither a Saint nor a Politician', *Young India 2* (12 May 1920).

Gandhi, Mohandas Karamchand, *True Education*. Ahmedabad: Navajivan Publishing House, 1962.

Grover, Verinder and Ranjana Arora, *Great Women of Modern India – Sucheta Kripalani: Her Contribution to Political, Economic and Social Development*. New Delhi: Deep and Deep Publications, 1993.

Haq, Ehsanul, *Education and Political Culture in India, The Limits of Schooling System and Political Socialisation*. New Delhi: Sterling Publishers, 1981.

Hartog, Philip, Some *Aspects of Indian Education, Past and Present*. London & Oxford: Oxford University Press, 1939.

Hasan, Sakina A., 'Women and Indian Nationalism, Culture Consciousness and Social Liberation'. Paper Presented to Seminar on *Women and Indian Nationalism*, at the Fourth National Conference of the Indian Association of Women's Studies, Chandigarh, October, 1986.

Hutchins, Francis, *Spontaneous Revolution: The Quit India Movement*. Delhi: Manohar, 1971.

Hutheesing, Krishna, *Jail Ke Ve Din*. Kashi (Varanasi): Mudran Gyan Mandal Yantralaya, 1944.

Hutheesing, Krishna, *With No Regrets: An Autobiography*. Bombay: Padma Publications, 1944.

Hutheesing, Krishna, *We Nehrus*. Bombay: Pearl Books, 1967.

Jain, Devaki (ed.), *Indian Women*. New Delhi: Publications Division, Government of India, 1975.

Jones, Kenneth W., *Socio-Religious Reform Movements in British India*. Cambridge: Cambridge University Press, 1989.

Joshi, Binapani, *Uttarakhand ki Samajik Hulchalon mein Mahilaon ki Bhumika*. in *Smarika*, Compendium on Freedom Fighters of Almora District. Almora: Almora Publications, 1981.

Joshi, K.L. and P.D. Shukla, 'Women and Education in India', in *Women and Education*. Paris: UNESCO, 1953, pp. 85–202.

Joshi, Pushpa (ed.), *Gandhi on Women, Collection of Mahatma Gandhi's Writings and Speeches on Women*. New Delhi: Centre for Women's Development Studies, 1988.

Joshi, Sudha, *Kurmanchal Kesari*. Agra: Chaturvedi Prakashan Samiti, 1970.

Kalhan, Promilla, *Kamala Nehru, An Intimate Biography*. New Delhi: Vikas Publishing House, 1973.

Karlekar, Malavika, 'Women's Nature and Access to Education', in Karuna Chanana (ed.), *Socialization, Education and Women: Explorations in Gender Identity*. Hyderabad: Orient Longman, 1988, pp. 129–165.

Kasturi, Leela and Vina Mazumdar, 'Women and Indian Nationalism: Some Questions', in Kasturi, Leela and Vina Mazumdar (eds), *Women and Indian Nationalism*. New Delhi: Vikas Publishing House, 1994, pp. xxv–lxii.

Kaur, Manmohan, *Role of Women in the Freedom Struggle, 1857–1947*. Delhi: Sterling Publishers, 1968.

Kishwar, Madhu, 'Arya Samaj and Women's Education – Kanya Mahavidyalaya, Jalandhar', in Review of Women's Studies, *Economic and Political Weekly*, Vol. XXI, No. 17, April 26, 1986 (pp. WS-9 – WS-24).

Kumar, Krishna, *Political Agenda of Education: A Study of Colonialist and Nationalist Ideas*. New Delhi: Sage, 1991.

Lateef, Shahida, *Muslim Women in India, Political and Private Realities: 1890s–1980s*. New Delhi: Kali for Women, 1990.

Lateef, Shahida, 'The Indian Women's Movement and National Development: An Overview', in Gail Minault (ed.), *The Extended Family, Women and Political Participation in India and Pakistan*. Delhi: Chanakya Publications, 1981.

Majumdar, R.C. (ed.), *Struggle for Freedom* (Volume 11 of *The History and Culture of the Indian People)*. Bombay: Bharatiya Vidya Bhawan, 1969.

Mayhew, Arthur, *The Education of India: A Study of British Educational Policy in India 1835–1920 and of its Bearing on National Life and Problems in India Today*. London: Faber & Gwyer, 1926.

Mazumdar, Vina, 'Education and Women's Equality', *Journal of Education and Social Change* [Journal of the Indian Institute of Education, Pune], Vol. 2, October–December, 1987.

Mazumdar, Vina, 'Education and Rural Women – Towards an Alternative Perspective', *Occasional Paper No. 11*, Centre for Women's Development Studies, 1988.

McCully, Bruce T., *English Education and the Origins of Indian Nationalism*. New York: Columbia University Press, 1940.

Menon, Visalakshi, *From Movement to Government: The Congress in the United Provinces, 1937–42*. New Delhi: Sage Publications, 2003.

Menon, Visalakshi, *Indian Women and Nationalism: The UP Story*. New Delhi: Shakti Books, Har-Anand Publications, 2003.

Meston. William, *Indian Education Policy: Its Principles and Problems*. Madras: Christian Literature Society, 1936.

Metcalf, Thomas R., *The Aftermath of Revolt, India 1857–1870*. Princeton: Princeton University Press, 1964.

Minault, Gail, *Secluded Scholars: Women's Education and Muslim Social Reform in Colonial India*. Delhi: Oxford University Press, 1999.

Mukherjee, Haridas and Uma, Mukherjee, *the Origins of The National Education Movement (1905–1910)*. Calcutta: Jadavpur University, 1957.

Nagar, Sandhya (Archival Officer, State Archives), 'Contribution of Women of Allahabad in the Freedom Struggle'. U.P. State Archives, Lucknow (unpublished, n.d.).

Naik, J.P., *Elementary Education in India: The Unfinished Business.* Bombay: Asia Publishing House, 1966.

Nanda, B.R., *The Nehrus: Motilal and Jawaharlal.* London: George Allen and Unwin, 1965.

Nanda, B.R. (ed.), *Indian Women from Purdah to Modernity.* New Delhi: Vikas Publishing House, 1966.

Nanda, B.R., *Gandhi: Pan-Islamism, Nationalism and Imperialism in India.* Delhi: Oxford University Press, 1989.

Nehru, Jawaharlal (ed.), *A Bunch of Old Letters: Being mostly written to Jawaharlal Nehru and some written by him.* (New Edition, with an Introduction by Sunil Khilnani). New Delhi: Penguin/Viking, 2005.

Nehru, Jawaharlal, *An Autobiography.* New Delhi: Oxford University Press, 1980.

Nehru, Shyam Kumari (ed.), *Our Cause: A Symposium on Indian Women.* Allahabad: Kitabistan, 1952.

Nurullah, Syed and J.P. Naik, *A Students' History of Education in India, 1800–1947.* Bombay: Macmillan and Co., 1951.

Oldenberg, Veena Talwar, *The Making of Colonial Lucknow, 1856–1877.* Princeton: Princeton University Press, 1984.

Owen, H.F., 'Towards Nation-wide Agitation and Organisation: The Home Rule Leagues, 1915–1918', in D.A. Low (ed.), *Soundings in Modern South Asian History.* Berkeley: University of California Press, 1968, pp 159–195.

Pande, Malabika, *Gandhi's Vision of Social Transformation.* Jaipur: Rawat Publications, 2011.

Pande, Vinaya Chandra and Sunit Singh (ed.): *Independence Movement and Uttar Pradesh.* New Delhi: A.P.H. Publishing Corporation, 2000.

Pandey, B.N. (ed.), *A Centenary History of the Indian National Congress 1885–1985*, 3 Vols. New Delhi: Vikas (for the All-India Congress Committee), 1985.

Pandey, Gyanendra, *The Ascendancy of the Congress in Uttar Pradesh, 1926-34: A Study in Imperfect Mobilisation.* Delhi: Oxford University Press, 1978. This work has been revised and re-issued in 2002 as *The Ascendancy of the Congress in Uttar Pradesh: Class, Community and Nation in Northern India, 1926–1940,* by Anthem Press, London.

Pandit, Vijaya Lakshmi, *The Scope of Happiness: A Personal Memoir.* New Delhi: Vikas Publishing House Private Ltd, 1979.

Panigrahi, D.N. (ed.), *Economy, Society and Politics in Modern India.* New Delhi: Vikas, 1985.

Patel, Sujata, 'Construction and Reconstruction of Woman in Gandhi'. *Economic and Political Weekly,* 23(8), 1988 (327–387).

Pathak, Shekhar, 'The begar abolition movements in British Kumaun'. *Indian Economic & Social History Review,* Vol. 28, No. 3: pp. 261–279.

Radha Kumar, *The History of Doing: An Illustrated Account of Movements for Women's Rights and Feminism in India, 1800–1990.* New Delhi: Zubaan, 1993.

Rao, Uma, *Kamala Nehru.* Unpublished monograph, sponsored by the Kamala Nehru Trust, New Delhi, n.d.

Rao, Uma, *Some Aspects of Women's Education in U.P.,* Unpublished Monograph. Shimla: Indian Institute of Advanced Study, 1991.

Reeves, P.D., B.D. Graham and J.M. Goodman, *Handbook to Elections in Uttar Pradesh, 1920–1951.* New Delhi: Manohar Book Service, 1975.

Ruben, David (trans.), *Widows, Wives and other Heroines: Twelve Stories by Premchand.* Delhi: OUP, 1998.

Sangari, Kumkum and Sudesh Vaidya (eds), *Recasting Women: Essays in Indian Colonial History,* New Delhi: Kali for Women, 1989 — specifically, Partha Chatterjee, 'The Nationalist Resolution of the Women's Question', pp 233–253; and Kapil Kumar, 'Rural Women in Awadh, 1917–1947: Baba Ram Chandra and the Women's Question', pp. 337–369.

Saradamoni, K., 'Women and Development', *in* C. Sheshadri and J.L. Pandey (eds), *Population Education: A National Source Book,* Vol. II. New Delhi: NCERT, 1991.

Sarkar, Sumit, *Modern India 1885–1947*. Delhi: Macmillan, 1983.

Sarkar, Sumit, *Swadeshi Movement in Bengal, 1903–08*. New Delhi: Peoples Publishing House, 1977.

Sayeed, S.M., 'Women's Participation in U.P. Politics – A Study of Political Attitudes and Performance of the Women Members of the U.P. Assembly'. *Indian Journal of Political Science,* Vol. 32, No. 2, 1971: pp. 213–231.

Sen, Amiya P., *Social and Religious Reform: The Hindus of British India*. New Delhi: Oxford University Press, 1985.

Sen, J.M., *History of Elementary Education in India*. Calcutta: Calcutta Book Co, 1941.

Sen, S.N., *History of the Freedom Movement in India (1857-1947)*. New Delhi: New Age International, 1997.

Sitaramayya, B. Pattabhi, *The History of the Indian National Congress (1885–1935)*. Madras, The Working Committee of the Congress, 1935.

Singh, Yogendra, *Modernization of Indian Tradition: A Systemic Study of Social Change.* Faridabad: Thomson Press (India) Publication Division, 1973.

Smarika, Compendium on Freedom Fighters of Almora District. Almora: District Coordination Committee, 1975.

Smarika, Compendium on Women Freedom Fighters of Agra. Agra: Vanita Vikas, Golden Anniversary Number, 1998.

Srinivas, M.N., *Social Change in Modern India*. Berkeley: University of California Press, 1966.

Taneja, Anup, *Gandhi, Women, and the National Movement, 1920-47*. New Delhi: Har-Anand Publications, 2005.

Thakur, Bharti, *Women in Gandhi's Mass Movements*. New Delhi: Deep and Deep Publications, 2006.

Thapar-Bjorkert, Suruchi, *Women in the Indian National Movement: Unseen Faces and Unheard Voices, 1930–42*. New Delhi: Sage Publications India, 2006.

NEWSPAPERS & JOURNALS

Aaj, Varanasi. Files available at the (Kashi) Nagari Pracharini Sabha, Varanasi.

Abhyudaya, Allahabad. Files available on Microfilm, Nehru Memorial Museum and Library, New Delhi.

Chaand, Hindi journal published by the Indian Press, Allahabad. Files available at Hindi Sahitya Sammelan Sangrahalaya, Allahabad.

Economic and Political Weekly, A Sameeksha Trust Publication, Mumbai.

Indian Annual Register (Annual Digest of Public Affairs of India). Reprinted edition for the period 1919–1947, Nehru Memorial Museum and Library, New Delhi. [Digital edition accessible at the Digital Library of India, http://www.dli.ernet.in]

National Herald, Lucknow. Files available on microfilm, Nehru Memorial Museum and Library, New Delhi.

Satyagraha Samachar, Hindi Daily, issued by Satyagraha Committee of Prayag. Edited by Baijnath Kapoor, and printed at the Abhyudaya Press, Allahabad, 1930. Files available at U.P. State Archives, Lucknow.

Stree Darpan, Hindi journal of Allahabad. Files available at Hindi Sahitya Sammelan Sangrahalaya, Allahabad.

Shakti, Weekly, Almora. Files available in the office of *Shakti*, Lala Bazaar, Almora.

The Leader, Allahabad. Files available in the Allahabad University Library and on Microfilm, Nehru Memorial Museum and Library, New Delhi.

LIST OF PERSONS INTERVIEWED

1. Kamla Bahuguna, Nationalist Activist, Allahabad, November 1996.
2. Swaroop Kumari Bakshi, Freedom Fighter, Lucknow, March 1998.

3. Saroj Gaurihar, Freedom Fighter, Agra, August 1999.

4. Snehlata Joshi, Nationalist Activist of Nainital, Haldwani, June 1998.

5. Pratibha Malaviya, Allahabad, June 1996, regarding her mother Ketaki Bhatta *alias* Saraswati Devi, Freedom Fighter of Allahabad.

6. Kalavati Misra, Freedom Fighter, Allahabad, February 1996.

7. Nityanand Misra, Historian and Teacher, Almora, June 1998.

8. Raj Rani Nishad, Freedom Fighter, Allahabad, March 1996.

9. Bhagwati Paliwal, Freedom Fighter, Agra, July 1999.

10. Hemlata Pande (daughter-in-law of *Kurmanchal Kesari* Badri Datt Pande), Almora, June 1998.

11. Cecilia Phillips, former Director of Women's Education, U.P., Allahabad, October 1997 (regarding women's mobilization in Lucknow during the freedom movement).

12. Mohan Lal Sah, Advocate, Almora, June 1998.

13. Manorama Shukla, *Vanar Sena* activist, Allahabad, December 1996.

14. Vinodini Sinha, Freedom Fighter, Allahabad, January 1980 (Dr Uma Rao).

15. Lakshmi Kant Verma, Litterateur, Allahabad, June 1996.

16. Savitri Wattal, *Vanar Sena* activist, Allahabad, July 1998.

Index